audreystyle

audreystyle

Introduction by
HUBERT DE GIVENCHY

Pamela Clarke Keogh

HarperCollins*Publishers*

DESIGNED BY SUSI OBERHELMAN

ISBN 0-06-019329-8

06 07 08 IM 11

For my mother,
Julia Clarke Keogh,
the most stylish woman I know

And for Patricia

contents

HAVING HAD THE PRIVILEGE of knowing Audrey Hepburn at the very beginning of her career, and having had the pleasure of making all her clothes, not only for all her contemporary films but also for herself, I am very proud to be able with these few words to render an homage to her in this book.

Audrey had a big personality. In the choice of her dresses, in wearing them with such elegance, chic, and simplicity. In a very personal way, she created her own look—"The Hepburn Style."

How proud and happy I am to have been able to work with and embellish my dear Audrey. She was "unique" and will always be so.

The Audrey Hepburn myth exists. It is here.

Givenchy

Hubert de Givenchy

prelude

IT'S 6:00 A.M. ON FIFTH AVENUE — and Audrey Hepburn is down on her luck as Holly Golightly; she's got a case of the mean reds that only a visit to Tiffany's can cure. Holding coffee in a paper cup and nibbling a danish, Miss Golightly envisions brighter days. The first thing that strikes us is her beauty. She has secrets, she is kind, she is worldly, she dreams of love. Dressed in a black dress slim as a line, her upper arms lithe and yearning, wearing paste jewelry as she contemplates the real thing, she looks in at a world more peaceful, more ordered, more glittering than her own — having breakfast at Tiffany's.

As a movie star, Audrey Hepburn is like us, only better. She has been to places we only dream of going, spoken words we long to say. She is Gigi, Ondine, a princess, a nun, Maid Marian, an angel. To this day we will follow her in any role, to the ends of the earth — even, perchance, to heaven.

AUDREY HEPBURN CAME OF AGE in the years following World War II, a time of vigorous economic growth, renewed optimism, and great change for women the world over. Women went to work in greater numbers, attended college, pursued their dreams. As always, fashion reflected this newfound freedom. In New York City's garment district, Hattie Carnegie invented what we now call ready-to-wear. Her designs were glamorous, sporty, modern. They reflected the best of the New World, what an American president in 1960 would refer to (with no apparent sense of irony) as "vigah."

With her blend of European elegance and American *sportif*, Audrey Hepburn stepped right into the middle of America's century with a look that was at once sophisticated and attainable. At a time when women began to look for role models who were not emblematic of men's fantasies but their own, Audrey crafted heroines who were courageous, vulnerable, beautiful, and strong in both their manner and their way of dress. While the classic film stars reclined in carefully posed studio shots, photographer Philippe Halsman caught the optimism of the new star, and youthful America, in his famous series of celebrity jumps—when he captured Audrey's gorgeous energy and infectious smile on film. As she jumps for joy in a full skirt and waist-tied white shirt, we see the Hollywood princess is a real girl after all.

With incomparable grace Audrey grasped hold of the popular imagination and has never shaken herself free. By example, she showed us another way to live: a modern, intelligent alternative that women from all walks of life could emulate. A distinct original, Audrey Hepburn encouraged women to discover and highlight their own strengths. Like Coco Chanel, she not only changed the way women dress, but forever altered the way they view themselves, broadening the definition of beauty and offering a worldly, unsubmissive, and less blatantly sexual model. As designer Vera Wang notes, "Audrey was one of the first modern women—it wasn't easy culturally to make your own way. The clothing she wore echoed her spirit and mind. In order for her to do it, she had to go out on a limb. It was pretty gutsy to turn her back on Hollywood, particularly coming out of the Jane Russell period of the 1950s."

Audrey's liberating message is still heard today as she continues to be held up as a forward-thinking feminine ideal. Before Jacqueline Onassis, before Gloria Steinem, Lena Horne, Princess Diana, or Oprah Winfrey, there was Audrey Hepburn, setting standards that have not been eclipsed. She not only defined her time, she transcended it.

When most stars of her era had faded into anonymity, Audrey continued to captivate for her entire life—and then some. In 1990 *People* magazine deemed her "One of the 50 Most Beautiful People in the World." In 1996, three years after her death, the influential English magazine *Harpers & Queen* conducted a poll to find the most fascinating women of our time. And in the number one spot? Audrey Hepburn.

Remarkably, Hepburn still affects fashion, that most fickle of arts. Her style is as timely as it is timeless; she is ingrained in our consciousness. Today's designers, movie stars, and glossy magazines celebrate looks directly descended from the work Audrey and Hubert de Givenchy collaborated on almost fifty years ago.

Audrey Hepburn is a wonderful role model not only because of her grace and generosity of spirit, but also because of her basic yet polished style. Many of her fashion lessons can be adapted for use right now; indeed, her influence on contemporary style is incomparable. "Women wear things today that they just take for granted," the designer Michael Kors observes, "but without Audrey Hepburn they probably wouldn't be wearing them." Grace Kelly had her Hermès bag, and Coco the little black dress, but Audrey popularized the gamine haircut, flat ballet shoes, the turtleneck, slim capri pants, extravagant dark glasses, cinched waists, three-quarter sleeves, and fitted shirts wrapped at the waist. Her personal style was so compelling that, as Cecil Beaton wrote in *Vogue,* "nobody ever looked like her before World War II . . . now thousands of imitations have appeared."

In this era of overhyped media stunts and endless celebrity profiles, when, as David Halberstam puts it, "there's all too much coverage of pseudo-events about extraordinarily inauthentic people doing inauthentic things,"

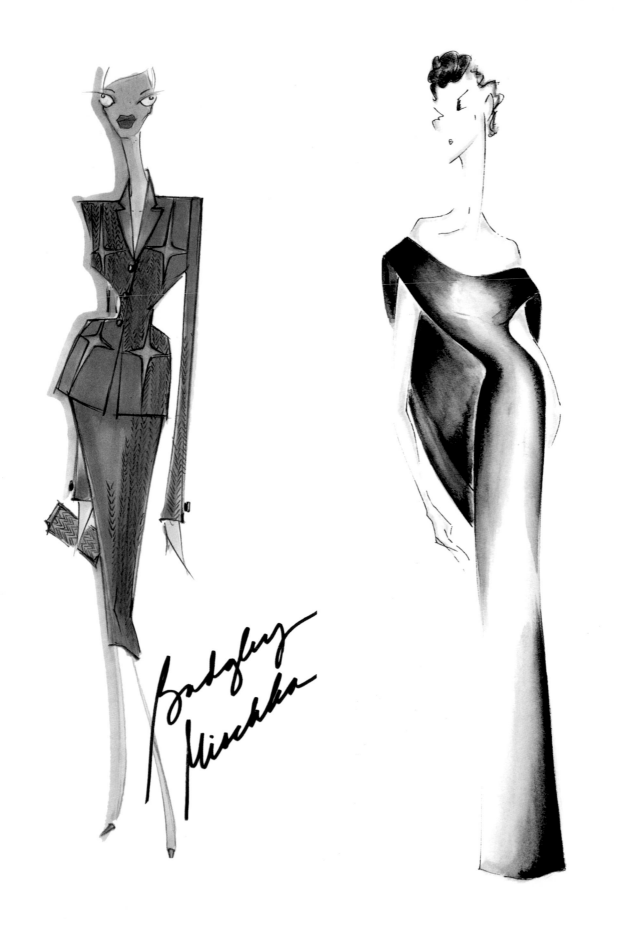

Audrey Hepburn is the real thing. As the century draws to a close, people are applauded for being notorious or, if they lack the imagination for this, merely crude. A person of lasting character, Audrey was the antithesis of today's modern celebrity. She was a great woman who had a style and grace that is now in short supply.

Clearly, there is a reason the world immediately fell in love with Audrey—and that we continue to do so each time we see her face on a magazine cover or watch her now-classic films. In Audrey we see a movie star who is down to earth yet compelling, contradictory yet steadfast. A courageous woman whose knees knocked together when she gave speeches in public. An instantly recognizable woman who was happiest at home with her family. A fashion icon with the simplest taste.

Audrey Hepburn became a star, and remains a star, because she never ceases to inspire us. As an actress she embodies our hopes, our dreams, and our heartache, and reflects them back to us more brilliantly than we could ever imagine. Audrey Hepburn's beauty, her vulnerability, and her courage are instinctive, visceral, electrifying. Most of all, she is honest—we believe who she is on the screen, we trust her.

As we shall see, Audrey's style evolved from her history; it was not manufactured by fashion photographers or a studio marketing department. Audrey was not groomed by Hollywood; rather, she taught Hollywood a thing or two about grooming. She awakened our dreams with her elegance and gamine charm. But those qualities were not lightly won. The deprivation Audrey knew as a child, her discipline, even the disappointment she suffered from her two husbands, all contributed to her luminosity.

As Billy Wilder described her after directing Audrey in *Love in the Afternoon*, "Ah, that unique lady. She's what the Latin calls *sui generis*. She's the original." Audrey Hepburn was an original, and her honesty shone forth on the screen. As *Harper's Bazaar* observed, "Hepburn attained stardom without compromising the qualities—innocence, earnestness, naturalness—that made her so appealing in the first place."

In the final analysis, the best word to describe Audrey and her style is *authentic*. Robert Wolders, the man who shared her life during her last thirteen years, found Audrey "secure in her values and early on found a level

where she felt and functioned best. Her personal style was a result of her unwillingness to compromise on these values and to focus on what is basic and real. She showed a good deal of stubbornness to outside influences, always insisting on what felt natural and comfortable. Her sense of appropriateness and decorum was happily mixed with a sense of irony and humor—not taking herself too seriously, but seriously enough."

Although there will be only—can be only—one Audrey Hepburn, this should not discourage us, since there is much to be learned from studying her life. By opening ourselves to the possibility of style, we can allow some Audrey into our lives, and grace not only our own being, but those around us. Which would, no doubt, please Miss Hepburn immeasurably.

Though she came to
there is no doubt they

Givenchy out of the blue, were made to meet.

DREDA MELE

> "There is not a woman alive who does not dream of looking like Audrey Hepburn."
>
> — HUBERT DE GIVENCHY

meeting monsieur givenchy

SPORTING CAPRI PANTS, a little white T-shirt, ballet slippers, and a gondolier hat she had picked up in Italy shooting *Roman Holiday*, Audrey stood for a moment in front of the stunning neo-Gothic mansion at 8 rue Alfred de Vigny, opposite the Parc Monceau. She wanted to be precisely on time for Monsieur Givenchy; after all, she knew from her mother, the baroness, that it was almost as ill mannered to arrive too early for an appointment as too late.

It was the summer of 1953, and Audrey had just been cast in her second major movie, *Sabrina*, with William Holden and Humphrey Bogart, where she plays a newly chic chauffeur's daughter caught between two feuding brothers. The director, Billy Wilder, sent her to Paris to pick out some designer originals to wear when Sabrina returns to America after her year abroad. She couldn't believe she was there. Audrey tilted her head back to study the ornate sandstone facade that had previously been owned by Meunier, the chocolate king. She smiled to herself—she was about to meet Hubert de Givenchy, the aristocratic six foot six devotee of Balenciaga who had opened his own design studio a year and a half before, and was already drawing raves for his understated, supremely elegant designs. Audrey knew of Givenchy's reputation—she followed fashion with the same intensity that some sports fans devote to baseball. In fact, Hubert had first come to her attention two years earlier, when he was

still an apprentice at the house of Schiaparelli, and she was in the South of France filming the light European comedy *Monte Carlo Baby*.

Her heart raced. Eight years before, in Holland during the war, she had been wearing homemade clothes, and now she was about to enter the rarified world of haute couture, where an embroidered blouse cost $3,000. It was almost too much to imagine.

It was time. Audrey was nervous about meeting Givenchy but forced herself past her fear. She straightened her shoulders and lifted her head, pulling herself up from the base of her spine as she learned in ballet class, making herself appear taller than her five foot seven inches. A doorman pushed open the heavy glass door to the atelier. "Mademoiselle?" *Roman Holiday* would not be released in America for a month, so Audrey could walk the streets of Paris—or anywhere, for that matter—unrecognized. She smiled at the doorman and stepped inside. The air was hushed, calm with the fragrance of full-blown white lilies. Surely nothing bad could ever happen here.

"I'm here to see Monsieur Givenchy, please."

"Oui, Mademoiselle," the doorman said, and motioned for her to go upstairs. With a short skip, Audrey took the steps two at a time.

Darting up the marble stairs, Audrey had no way of knowing that this seemingly fated fashion meeting with Givenchy almost didn't take place. At first she had considered Cristobal Balenciaga to design her French costumes for *Sabrina*, but no one, least of all Gladys de Segonzac, married to the head of Paramount's Paris office, who arranged Audrey's trip to Paris, had the audacity to disturb him so close to the showing of his collection. Indeed, the loyalty of Balenciaga's followers was so absolute that Mrs. Paul Mellon took to her bed for two weeks, literally, when he announced he was closing his studio in 1968.

Then, Audrey suggested, what about Hubert de Givenchy? Mme. de Segonzac smiled. An *excellent* idea! It turned out she was a good friend of Hubert's, and offered to make the introduction. Segonzac then called Givenchy and implored him to meet with the young actress. Although he was rushing to prepare his own collection, Givenchy agreed. "One day, someone told me that Miss Hepburn was coming to Paris to select some clothes for her new film. At the time I had never heard of Audrey Hepburn. I only knew of Katharine Hepburn. Of course I was happy to receive Katharine Hepburn," he remembers. When introduced to Audrey, Givenchy graciously hid his disappointment. "My first impression of her was that she was like a very fragile animal. She had such beautiful eyes and she was so skinny, so thin. . . . And no makeup. She was charming."

Hubert was twenty-six years old when they met, Audrey less than two years younger. Like brother and sister, they developed a friendship that would last the rest of her life. They had similar personalities—Hubert habitually rose at seven, Jeannette, his faithful secretary, was at her desk by eight, with his models made up, coiffed, and ready by nine. It was, he said, merely "a matter of discipline" to behave so conscientiously. Working fourteen hours a day, sketching, conducting fittings, and inspecting fabric, Givenchy had tremendous physical energy and intelligence as well as Gallic refinement. Dreda Mele, the *directrice* of Givenchy, remembers how similar Audrey and Hubert were: rigorous, well organized, concentrated on their work, and "behaving so well at every moment of life."

In Audrey, Hubert met someone who loved clothes (and, as they would discover, gardens) almost as much as he did. As a schoolboy in France, where his family owned the Gobelin and Beauvais tapestry factories, his grandmother had rewarded his good grades by showing him her treasures—entire cabinets full of every kind of fabric, which left him dazzled. As a grown man, now a designer, he knew that fabric was where it all began, "the preamble to inspiration," as he put it. From his master, Balenciaga, Givenchy further learned: "Never work against the fabric, which has a life of its own." For Givenchy, the rich material of his craft had as much sensual appeal as a delicious meal or fine wine to a gourmand. "The allure, the odor of silk, the feel of a velvet, the crackle of a *satin duchesse*—what intoxication! The colors, the sheen of a faille, the iridescent side of a shot taffeta, the strength of a brocade, the caress of a velvet panel—what bliss! What extraordinary sensuality!"

But when Hubert first laid eyes on Audrey, he had no time to help her, no matter how compelling her gaze. There was the collection to prepare, just weeks away, and so much to be done. Audrey pleaded—if he couldn't design the clothes for the film (and from the looks of things, that was *impossible*), perhaps he would allow her to find something ready-made from a previous show?

Hubert shrugged. What could one do with this girl? With a smile and

a promise to hurry, Audrey darted through the bustling workroom, heading for the racks.

The first outfit Audrey tried on, a gray wool suit that had been modeled by Colette Cerf, fit almost perfectly, since they both had the same daunting twenty-inch waistline. The effect, the change in Audrey, was astonishing; Givenchy, for one, could not believe his eyes. This little ragamuffin—what did she say she was, an actress?—was suddenly transformed into a beauty to rival any of his mannequins.

"The way she moved in the suit, she was so happy," says Givenchy. "She said it was exactly what she wanted for the movie. Something magic happened—you could feel her excitement, her joy."

For her second choice Audrey discovered a white, fitted, strapless ball gown with a detachable train that enveloped her from the waist to the floor in a spray of organdy. Embroidered with a floral design of black silk thread and jet beads on the bodice, skirt, and train, the dress took one's breath away. This gamine stranger brought such life to the clothes. With her slender neck, thin-waisted body, and long legs, Givenchy saw that his clothes suited her perfectly.

For her final costume Audrey selected a black, ribbed-cotton-piqué dinner dress for Sabrina's date with Linus Larrabee. It was fitted through the waist with a full ballerina skirt that fell to the calf and a tiny bow at each shoulder. She particularly appreciated the way the neckline—*décolleté bateau*, it was called—hid what she considered her skinny collarbone, although she didn't confide this to Givenchy until later.

Audrey liked her outfits to have a bit of whimsy, to reveal some personality (hence, the straw boater); she enjoyed combining pieces in an unpredictable way. So she hunted around the workroom in search of just the right hat for the black dress. Her eye caught a snug-fitting cap with a spray of rhinestones—perfect! Looking at her, the seamstresses in their white smocks couldn't help but smile. She was *magnifique*!

Now intrigued by Audrey, Givenchy invited her to dinner at a bistro on the rue de Grenelle. Over coq au vin and a bottle of wine, they exchanged stories and Audrey told him of the war and her experiences in London and Hollywood. "I love clothes to where it is practically a vice," Audrey giggled, delicately tearing a piece of baguette. She also confided in him that with the first real money she made from *Roman Holiday*, she bought one of his coats, off the rack, anonymously, paying full price like any other fan. Hubert was charmed.

Although they could scarcely imagine what the coming years had in store for them, Audrey and Hubert recognized that they were part of a natural aristocracy, one that had nothing to do with money, power, or family placement and everything to do with talent, hard work, and a faith that somehow they would prevail. There was an ingrained grace about each of them that money could not buy.

In Hubert, Audrey found a best friend who shared her outlook on the world. It was like falling in love—perhaps even better. Like her ability to choose just the right ensemble, her sense that she could trust him was instinctive. Soon after they met she was calling him to tell him that she loved him, then hanging up the telephone. Her affection for Hubert never wavered. "There are few people I love more," she would later say. "He is the single person I know with the greatest integrity."

In the superstitious world of fashion, where Coco Chanel incorporated both her astrological sign (a lion) and a four-leaf clover into her work, many felt Audrey and Hubert were fated to meet. It certainly seemed that way. As Dreda Mele told *Vanity Fair*, "Audrey was always very definite in her taste and look. She came to him because she was attracted by the image he could give her. And she entered that dream totally. She entered into his dream too. They were made for each other."

WHILE AUDREY and Givenchy celebrated their newfound friendship, legendary costume designer Edith Head was back in Hollywood under the distinct impression that *she* was solely responsible for Hepburn's wardrobe. And Head rarely took a professional misstep. During her forty-four-year career (first at Paramount and then at Universal Studios), Head was a shrewd politician and infighter. One joke among the seamstresses in the costume department was that their boss would claim to have invented the skirt if she thought she could get away with it. Indeed, at the peak of her career it was written into her contract that Head was the only designer who could get credit on any Paramount picture. Billy Wilder remembers that he didn't choose her for *Sabrina*, she was automatically assigned to all first-class pictures at Paramount.

The scuttlebutt in Hollywood was that Edith wasn't a designer at all, she didn't even know how to *draw* properly—she just signed her large distinctive, looping signature at the bottom of someone else's sketch. But while she may have been a workmanlike designer, she had great people skills. At Paramount it was said that Edith was the only person who could be both "subservient and behave like a star." Leading ladies like Barbara Stanwyck, Carole Lombard, Grace Kelly, and Elizabeth Taylor gravitated toward the support and confidence she gave them, demanding to work with her. In a field full of prima donnas, Head chose to act more like a corporate executive than an artiste. She subtly made herself indispensable to those above her on the power chain. Whenever a star or an important executive's wife needed to borrow a dress to go to a premiere or a party at Romanoff's, Edith happily lent them something from costume.

When Audrey Wilder, Billy's wife, was working on *Salty O'Rourke* with Alan Ladd, Edith said, "Here's a black dress you can wear. We'll give you a fur piece." Audrey Wilder mentioned that she just happened to have bought a silver fox fur at Teitelbaum's, where the studios rented furs—for a hundred bucks down and forty a month. "Fine," said Edith. "I'll hire your stole for the picture." She even wrote out a contract: Silver fox—$50 a day. So while Mrs. Wilder was making about thirty-five dollars a day, her stole was making fifty. She paid off Teitelbaum's like that.

Audrey and Edith first worked together on *Roman Holiday*. At their initial meeting, Edith was enchanted by the young starlet (as well as amazed at her ability to consume a hot fudge sundae or four chocolate eclairs at one sitting). "I knew she would be the perfect mannequin for anything I would make." Edith immediately saw that Hepburn had a far better understanding of fashion and its requirements than other actresses, even going so far as to have a sketch pad imprinted with her outline to help with the designing of her costumes. "Audrey's fittings became the ten-hour, not the ten-minute variety," Head remembered. "She knew exactly how she wanted to look or what worked best for her, yet she was never arrogant or demanding. She had an adorable sweetness."

The adorably sweet girl may have been polite, but she was no pushover. Audrey knew exactly how she wanted to look and what worked for her, and even better, having just returned from Paris, knew the man to do it—Hubert de Givenchy. With her finely tuned instinct for fashion, Audrey suggested that Givenchy, unknown in America except in the most sophisticated echelons of society, design her clothes for *Sabrina*. Billy Wilder broke the news to Edith, making it appear as though it was his idea. Although she would demand, and receive, credit for all the costumes, she was actually relegated to designing Sabrina's ragamuffin, living-over-the-garage costume and a few minor things (the shorts and madras blouse she wears on her date with Linus Larrabee on his sailboat, for example). Head was heartbroken.

FRESH FROM COOKING SCHOOL in Paris, Sabrina is met at the Glen Cove train station by David Larrabee in his Nash-Healey convertible. Wearing a fine gray knife-cut suit that reveals her curves beneath the masculine wool, she is a far cry from the typical society girls one sees on the North Shore of Long Island. David wonders: Who *is* this mysterious beauty? And how does she know so much about him? Her *soigné* appearance includes exotically made-up eyes, a fringe of bangs peeking beneath her pale gray turban, white gloves, a stack of hard luggage, a poodle, and a magnetic, enigmatic aura. She has a secret she is not letting him in on, and the playboy is intrigued.

And so it is that audiences around the world, like David Larrabee, meet the new-and-improved Sabrina and are instantly smitten. When the credits roll, we see Edith Head was responsible for Miss Hepburn's wardrobe. Not much later we learn that Hubert de Givenchy designed the outfits we *really* loved, while Edith took credit for everything. In later years she would even claim to have created "*décolleté* Sabrina," the distinctive Givenchy neckline Audrey favored to hide her collarbone and reveal her strong shoulders.

Audrey and Givenchy's *Sabrina* collaboration caused an earthquake among the style conscious. Every woman, it seemed, wanted to be Audrey Hepburn. And if this proved impossible, they gladly mimicked her fashion. In fact, one lone copy of a Givenchy design for *Sabrina* began circulating even before the picture was released, and from a very surprising corner. Audrey Wilder had seen the sketches that Audrey had brought her husband from Paris. She took the one of the black cocktail dress to her mother, a superb seamstress who worked for all the studios. Her mother sewed a copy for her

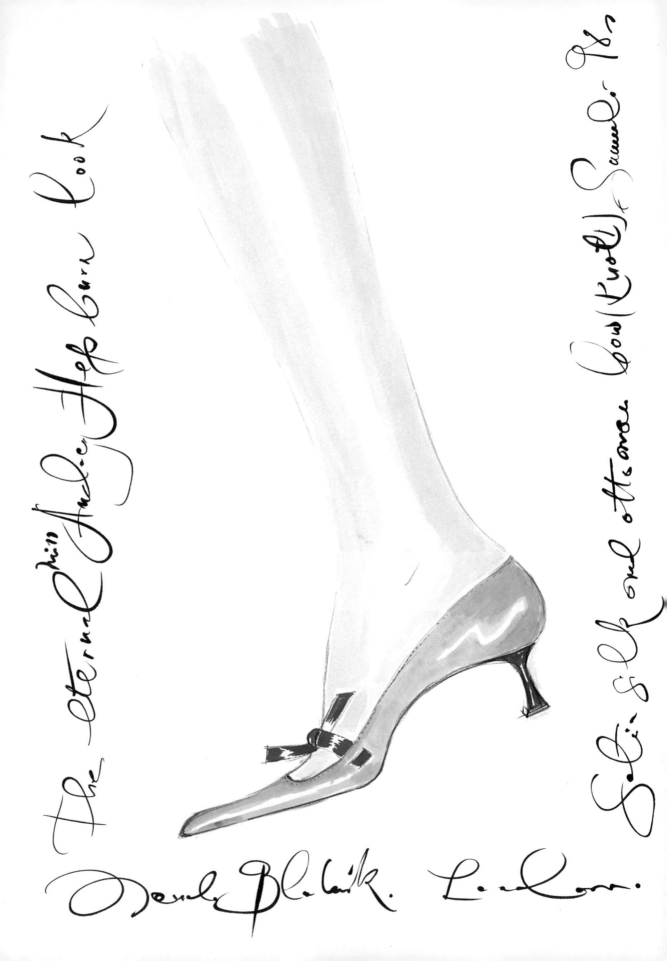

The eternal Audrey Hepburn Look

Satin silk and others one bow (knot) Suede 18s

Manolo Blahnik. London.

daughter, who wore it one evening. "That's not fair!" Billy exclaimed (although, he had to admit, she looked terrific in it). "The movie's not even out yet!"

But the wholehearted embrace of Audrey's style went further than the clothes on her back. "Everyone on the street was copying Audrey's hair," Dreda Mele recalls, "the way she moved, the way she spoke. Everyone wanted to look like Audrey Hepburn. They copied her for ten solid years after." And did Audrey realize her effect on fashion? "Well," exclaims Audrey Wilder, "when she saw an imitation of herself walking down the street—sure she did!"

Audrey invited Hubert to attend the premiere of *Sabrina*, in what was his first trip to Los Angeles. Sitting in the audience, Audrey was stung that Givenchy was not even included in the credits. Givenchy, for his part, was too polite to comment, saying it must have been an "oversight." Audrey, mortified, promised to make it up to him. She did. After their initial success, Givenchy and Audrey continued the longest running, most successful fashion collaboration in history. He designed her wardrobe in *Funny Face* (1957), *Love in the Afternoon* (1957), *Breakfast at Tiffany's* (1961), *Charade* (1963), *Paris When It Sizzles* (1964), and *How to Steal a Million* (1966), as well as the dress for her second wedding, her sons' christenings, and their christening gown.

Givenchy—who once said that "a woman does not simply wear a dress; she lives in it"—had a philosophy about style that ideally matched Audrey's, just as the pure line of his clothing perfectly complemented her classic silhouette. Givenchy recognized in Audrey all that was young, cultured, and rare, lending her a Parisian sophistication that distinguished her from other starlets of the day. The strength and confidence that his clothing gave her were almost psychological. "His are the only clothes in which I am myself," Audrey told reporters in 1956. "He is far more than a couturier, he is a creator of personality." In return for this support, Audrey willingly became the muse that inspired the house of Givenchy.

Together they developed the crisp lines, simple color, and extraordinary workmanship that defined Audrey Style. Without a doubt the friendship and artistic collaboration between Audrey and Hubert is one of the most important fashion pairings ever. Manolo Blahnik, the master shoe craftsman who recently revived the "Sabrina heel" in homage to Audrey's influence, feels that "the imprint of Miss Hepburn is absolutely, totally present, omnipresent forever.

Like it or not, she will be *the* most important look of the twentieth century."

Givenchy confirms that Audrey's elevation to one of the world's style leaders was no fluke. "She knew exactly what she wanted. She knew perfectly her visage and her body, their fine points and their faults. Later I tried to adapt my designs to her desires. She wanted a bare-shouldered evening dress modified to hide the hollows behind her collarbone. What I invented for her eventually became a style so popular that I named it '*décolleté* Sabrina.'"

Her friend Ralph Lauren, too, gives Audrey equal, if not more, credit in the Hepburn/Givenchy pairing. "I truly feel Audrey gave Givenchy a look. As time went on, they collaborated, but I think she picked what was Audrey out of Givenchy. The same for my clothes. She just picked from them what was right for her." Model Christy Turlington agrees with Lauren. "Givenchy made a lot of beautiful things, but the pieces you really remember are the things he did with her, and I think that has to do with what she brought out in him. Those are my favorite pieces. That was really quite a partnership, she wasn't just a muse—she was much more thoughtful than that in those designs."

With her distinctly individual look, Hepburn did something else, perhaps without fully realizing her impact at the time—she also broadened the boundaries of acceptable feminine beauty for the next decade. It should be remembered that choosing this modern style, no matter how current it looks today, was eminently radical on Audrey's part. In an age of the bouffant hairdo, tight skirts, tighter sweaters, Jane Russell (and the brassiere Howard Hughes designed for her), Audrey's boyish figure, cropped hair, and ballet slippers were the mark of a real individual.

Hepburn ushered in a fresh, forward-looking style that depended on the wearer knowing herself rather than on mimicking fashion. According to Vera Wang, "Audrey dressed contrary to Hollywood at that time, she dressed for herself. Her very singular style was a combination of things—her physique combined with the courage to go her own way, she was also able to recognize the genius of Givenchy. It wasn't one thing. The thing that strikes me about Audrey, still, is the courageousness of her personal style."

Audrey's friendship with Givenchy was central to her development as a woman and as an actress. There would be other designers in Audrey's life— Valentino when she lived in Rome, Ralph Lauren in the 1980s for daywear, she even wore Guess jeans when traveling for UNICEF—but none she loved so much as Hubert. Her relationship with him extended for more years than both her husbands combined. He served her as faithfully as any queen's consort. Later in life she asked him to be her *légataire testamentaire*, a mediator of her will.

After Audrey's death in 1993, the fashion world commented posthumously on their relationship with enough randomly malicious gossip to impress Josephine, Napoleon, and the entire court of Versailles. "She was entirely Givenchy's creation," says a prominent publicist. "Audrey knew what she wanted and took it from Hubert," snipes another designer known for his, shall we say, derivative work. Gregory Peck, for his part, believes that "in her sense of style— she knew what was good for her. You have to remember that Givenchy was serving Audrey's best interests. Her style was uniquely hers." Even Edith Head was dragged into the morass. "Edith never designed a thing for Audrey," confides Audrey Wilder, clearly in a position to know. Then, who did? "Hubert! He did everything!" she says with a short laugh, implying, *but you already knew that, didn't you?* "Hubert sent her sketches and she made the clothes. She got the credit because Hubert couldn't join the Costumer's Union."

Audrey and Hubert. Givenchy and Hepburn. Who led and who followed? Does it matter? In the end, as in the best love affairs, the only ones who knew the truth about the relationship between Hubert and Audrey were Hubert and Audrey. One need only see them walking together along the Seine, two lions in winter, Hubert, his arm protectively around Audrey, sheltering her as she confides in him. Like the most compelling romances, Audrey and Hubert are linked together in our minds forever.

three easy pieces

Amazingly, for all the fashion ruckus she raised, Audrey borrowed just three pieces from Givenchy's spring/summer collection of 1953 to wear in *Sabrina*. When she showed up practically unannounced on his doorstep, he was furiously preparing the winter collection (to be shown in July, as is typical in the fashion world). Hubert explained that he would not be able to help her, he simply could not spare anyone.

Undaunted, Audrey searched the racks containing last season's collection, found a suit, a dress, and a ball gown, raided his workshop for appropriate hats to go with two of the outfits, and stunned the world.

The Glen Cove Suit—This was the first suit Audrey saw after she introduced herself to Givenchy, and what a winner. *Vanity Fair* describes it as "an Oxford-gray wool-ottoman *tailleur* with a cinch-waisted, double-breasted scoop-neck jacket and a slim, calf-length vented skirt." Audrey called it "jazzy." Translation: *fabulous*.

The White Ball gown—Number 808 of the '53 spring/summer collection was called "Inez de Castro." Givenchy sketched it as an ankle-length skirt and matching jacket, with a black, scoop-neck, three-quarter-sleeve top. Audrey's version was a strapless dress with detachable overskirt. A stunner. For the best Cinderella moment in cinematic history, Audrey shows up at the Larrabee

mansion in this, and boy, do they regret treating her like a nobody over the garage all those years. William Holden nabs a pair of champagne flutes, cues the orchestra to play "Isn't It Romantic?" (heard practically ad nauseam throughout the film because Paramount owned the rights and wanted its money's worth), and hightails it out to the tennis court with the chauffeur's daughter. A dress to change your life.

The Denouement Date Dress—Insecure about his diminishing role and William Holden's friendship with the director, Humphrey Bogart was a terror on the set. For this he was banned from evening cocktails and threatened with being written out of the script if he didn't behave himself. Still, seeing Audrey in this dress, you'd think Sabrina and Linus really do love each other. A black cocktail dress, fitted through the waist with a perky bow on each shoulder, it was cut deeply in the back and armholes, and featured a neckline that would forever after be called "*décolleté Sabrina*." P.S. Don't take Edith's word for it, this dress has Givenchy written all over it. According to a production memo, Audrey bought all three outfits herself from Hubert so Paramount would not have to pay customs or give Givenchy credit since they were now considered part of Hepburn's personal wardrobe. In case you're wondering, the black dress cost $560.

I wanted to
and a choreographer

be Margot Fonteyn
as well.

A H

"She had that rare thing, audience authority,
that makes everybody look at you."

— CATHLEEN NESBITT

ingenue

IT WAS JUNE 1951, and the austere marble lobby of Monte Carlo's Hôtel de Paris was littered with cameras, cables, and directorial chaos as *Monte Carlo Baby* was being shot. An unknown actress danced lightly, instinctively, to entertain herself between shots. An aged, imposing woman in a wheelchair happened to see her and was charmed. "I could not take my eyes away," Colette remembered. *"That* is my Gigi!" she declared imperiously to her entourage. "Who is that creature?" She demanded an introduction. Colette had just glimpsed Audrey Hepburn and was certain that this complete unknown should star in the Broadway version of her novel *Gigi*.

What Colette responded to was not the stranger's costume (striped silk pantaloons, at the moment), or her acting ability in this very light French comedy, but rather her aura, her attitude—something that, unfortunately, all the designer clothes in the world cannot bestow upon you. While Audrey's singular beauty and Givenchy's stunning designs brought Hepburn to the world's attention, it was her "inner style" that ensured she would not be forgotten. Novelists by their very nature have a rich interior life, and perhaps Colette recognized a kindred spirit in Audrey. Perhaps, too, this leap of imagination is what was needed for anyone to envision Audrey in her first starring role on Broadway.

At Colette's insistence, Audrey went to New York City, where, after six weeks of stressful rehearsal, she opened in *Gigi*. The reviews were lukewarm,

but audiences gave her standing ovations. The producers, who had despaired at Audrey's inability to project her voice and even tried to replace her two weeks earlier, discovered they had a hit on their hands. The impossibly young-looking doe-eyed girl with the fringe of dark hair had captured Broadway. The morning after opening night, Audrey climbed a ladder and placed the letter "A" in front of "UDREY HEPBURN" as a *Daily News* photographer snapped away. Her name was above the title—a star was born, and Hollywood soon beckoned.

OF COURSE, OVERNIGHT SUCCESS is never overnight. Behind early public acclaim are years of heartache, misguided attempts to get somewhere (often anywhere), talent, faith, and luck. So it follows that as a young woman, Audrey possessed a style that was embryonic, instinctive, as she made her way in the world with little more than hope and an unfailing belief in herself. What is most intriguing about Audrey at this stage of her life is how she already had much of what eventually constituted her appeal.

Nickolas Dana, who danced with Audrey in *High Button Shoes*, the American hit musical with Jule Styne music and Jerome Robbins choreography that was brought to London in 1948, remembers Audrey's nascent style. As a struggling chorus girl, it seemed she had "one skirt, one blouse, one pair of shoes, and a beret, but she had fourteen scarves. What she did with them week by week you wouldn't believe. She'd wear the little beret on the back of her head, on one side, on the other side—or fold it in two and make it look very strange. She had the gift, the flair of how to dress." While Audrey acquired more gloss, confidence, and certainly acclaim with time, the qualities that drew people like Colette to her were there from the start.

If "regal" was one of the more popular adjectives used to describe Hepburn in the coming years, it may not have been without good reason. Audrey was born Edda Kathleen van Heemstra Hepburn-Ruston in Brussels on May 4, 1929. Her mother was a Dutch baroness whose own aspirations of being an actress and opera singer were discounted by her family because of their place in society. Audrey's father, Joseph Hepburn-Ruston, was an Anglo-Irish businessman. The Hepburn-Rustons had a difficult marriage, made worse by Joseph's strong Nazi inclinations, alcohol abuse, and his eventual decision to channel some of his in-laws' wealth toward fascist causes.

In May 1935 Ruston did the unthinkable: He walked out on his wife and six-year-old daughter. Audrey called her father's disappearance "the most traumatic event in my life." Her mother's hair turned white overnight. Audrey's recollection of her own response and the memory of her mother's is haunting: "You look into your mother's face, and it's covered with tears, and you're terrified. You say to yourself, 'What's going to happen to me?' The ground has gone out from under you. . . . He really left. He just went out and never came back." In spite of this loss, Audrey continued to harbor great love for her father and mourned his absence as long as she lived.

Despite her father's disappearance, there was joy in Audrey's young life. Growing up in the Dutch town of Arnhem during World War II, she had always loved ballet, which she began studying at the age of eleven. Dance was an escape for Audrey, a means to an end, an attempt to find beauty in an unkind world. As chaotic as the war years were, she always continued with her lessons. It gave a center to her world. In fact, she gathered up neighborhood children and gave them lessons at her grandfather's home, installing a barre in his large entrance hall with its black and white marble floor. "I gave classes for all ages," she remembered, "I accepted what was about a dime a lesson. We worked to a gramophone wound by hand." By 1944, as the Germans marched across Europe, Audrey was dancing endless hours in shoes that were worn to shreds but impossible to replace. Finally, she resorted to the only painful alternative—wooden ones.

But even the rigorous beauty of ballet could not keep reality at bay. The van Heemstra family was rumored to be of part-Jewish ancestry, and a favorite uncle and cousin were executed as enemies of the Third Reich. Occupying forces confiscated Audrey's ancestral home and bank accounts. Though just a child, she distributed anti-Nazi literature during the war and barely escaped capture by the Germans.

Audrey never forgot the suffering she and others endured under the Nazis. At fifteen she was in Holland during what became known as "the hunger winter"—the last winter of the war, 1945, where so many died of starvation and a tuberculosis epidemic that there was a shortage of caskets. She once spoke, famously, of eating tulip bulbs and trying to make bread from grass. Many days she had only water to drink, and drank a great deal of it in an attempt to

feel full, or went to bed in the afternoon to conserve her strength. After witnessing her mother's struggle to find food for the two of them, Audrey "willed" herself to do without it, beginning a lifelong habit of not eating during times of stress.

By the time Holland was liberated, Audrey was five foot six, weighed ninety pounds, and was afflicted with anemia, asthma, jaundice, and other diseases stemming from poor diet. Having suffered from varying degrees of malnutrition from the age of eleven through sixteen, Audrey's metabolism would always be affected by her traumatic adolescence. And although she eventually grew another inch and weighed one hundred ten pounds as an adult, she struggled, always, to keep weight on. While her famous "gamine" figure would become celebrated in the coming years, it was, in fact, a combination of genes (she said she had the exact same figure as her father's mother) and tragic circumstance.

But perhaps more significant—and lasting—than any physical deprivation, Audrey paid an emotional price for her childhood experiences. In a television interview in 1990, Phil Donahue asked Audrey if living under the Nazis had left her insecure. "That is not what left me insecure," she answered. "My father leaving us is what left me insecure. It has stayed with me through my own relationships. When I fell in love and got married, I lived in constant fear of being left. . . . Whatever you love most, you fear you might lose."

The abrupt departure of one's father, the terror of the Nazis, and wartime deprivation are not such history to recover from easily. If, in Cecil Beaton's famous portraits Audrey's luminous eyes reflect joy, there is always a shadow too. Audrey knew about the wolf at the door. A baroness's daughter, she had scrounged the hard November ground for something to eat. She knew firsthand what it was to lose everything: She had seen her indomitable mother weep with fear. Audrey's childhood made her both stronger and more vulnerable, giving her an extra human dimension—it certainly set her apart from most Americans of her generation. As her friend Roger Caras observed, "You come out of her kind of background one of two ways, hard or soft. She came out soft." Polly Mellen, who would work with the young Audrey on Richard Avedon fashion shoots for *Harper's Bazaar*, agrees. "There was a great softness to Audrey. To be in that business and have that softness is hard, very very hard—it's dog eat dog. I think there was a core of certainty to her. I think she knew herself because of her family, where she came from. She had a history, a background."

Adolf Hitler committed suicide on April 30, 1945. On May 4, 1945, Audrey's sixteenth birthday, Holland was liberated. It was, she recalled, "the best birthday present I ever had!" A few nights later, Canadian troops plugged a projector into an electric generator in the town square and, to the delight of Audrey and her teenage friends, gave an outdoor screening of a Hollywood film, the first they had seen since the war. As news of the outside world returned along with thoughts of the future, Audrey sensed a need to reinvent herself. Painfully shy, with no ambition except to make a living for herself and her mother, she aspired to be a ballet dancer. (After winning an Oscar for *Sabrina*, she confided that it was, after all, "easier to be a shy dancer than a shy actress.") Soon after, with one hundred pounds between them, Audrey and her mother left for London, where the baroness sensed there would be greater opportunities for her daughter.

THE BARONESS'S WILL was formidable, and the bond between her and her daughter—for better or worse—was intense. While constructing a life for them in London, Ella did all she could to help Audrey. She gave manicures, worked in a flower shop, and eventually became landlady of an apartment house at 65 South Audley Street in Mayfair to pay for Audrey's ballet lessons, resting her considerable hopes on her daughter's slim shoulders. Audrey would go far—further, perhaps, than either of them could imagine. A great deal would be asked of her along the way. For the moment, though, she and her mother were simply trying to survive, and Audrey was grateful for her mother's sacrifices. And although they did not share any physical resemblance, in her own way Ella contributed to the development of Audrey's style. "My mother," Audrey once said, perhaps only half seriously, "taught me to stand straight, sit erect, use discipline with wine and sweets, and to smoke only six cigarettes a day."

Despite their closeness, there was occasional tension between the two women. When she herself was young, Ella wanted to be thin, beautiful, and an actress. "Now, isn't it ironic," she once confided to a friend, "that I should have a daughter who's all three?" While Audrey's mother was proud of her daughter's success, she wasn't surprised by it—she expected nothing less. Yet, like many mothers, she found it difficult to tell her daughter that she loved her. So Ella

expressed her affection in other ways—by channeling her will into Audrey's advancement, doing all she could to push her forward. As a friend of Audrey's noted, "Without Audrey's mother there would never have been an Audrey."

The friction between the two women may have been one of temperament. Audrey always had a deep need for love and affection—she admitted as much herself. So it must have been troubling for this sensitive girl to have been raised by a woman who had difficulty expressing warm emotions. As Audrey said in a rare self-revelatory comment, "It is true that I had an extraordinary mother, [but] she herself was not a very affectionate person in the sense that I today consider affection. She's a fabulous mother, but she came from an era . . . of great discipline, of great ethics. Lot of love within her, not always able to show it. And very strict. I would search all over the place to find somebody who would cuddle me, you know? And I found it in my aunts, in my nannies. That was something that stayed with me."

While the Baroness Ella van Heemstra was proud of Audrey and her accomplishments, she could never convey this simple fact to her only daughter. "Considering that you have no talent, it's really extraordinary where you've gotten" was as close as she came to a compliment. Audrey herself admitted that her self-effacement, which her mother surely encouraged, was linked to her "enormous need of not only receiving [love], but desperately to give it, an enormous *need* to give it!"

Audrey even hugged and kissed her agent, Michael Black, once on each cheek, upon meeting him for the first time. To kiss your agent—in Hollywood no less! A man who would gladly—heck, *daily*—shake hands with the devil at the Universal commissary and then take 15 percent off the top. (Which is not to say he didn't deserve it. Commenting on Audrey's inimitable style, Mr. Black observed, in his own perhaps inimitable way, that Audrey would look good in *lint*.)

Her mother's firm lessons stayed with Audrey throughout her life. In 1991, with the world at her feet, she accepted an award given to her by the Film Society at Lincoln Center. Clad in a glorious Givenchy gown with brocade jacket, she smiled broadly to the crowd and said, "As a child, I was taught that it was bad manners to bring attention to yourself, and to never, *ever* make a spectacle of yourself." The audience laughed, thinking Audrey was being her typically modest self. Little did they know how closely she held this truth.

IN 1948 AUDREY WAS AWARDED a modest grant to attend Marie Rambert's famous ballet school in London, where Nijinsky had once studied. At the time Audrey joined her "Ballet Club," Rambert was in her sixties, nearing the end of an illustrious career, during which she founded the company that would evolve into the Sadler's Wells and, later, the Royal Ballet. While there, the girl who was baptized Edda Kathleen van Heemstra Hepburn-Ruston began to call herself, simply, Audrey Hepburn.

In almost every image we have of Audrey during these early years in London, she wears ballet tights and slippers. She thought of herself as a dancer. More than any single art form, ballet provided the underpinning for Audrey's look. Through ballet she honed her considerable powers of discipline and concentration. Through ballet she learned the rigors of dedication, the beauty of self-denial, and the paramount importance of the silhouette. These childhood lessons stayed with her always; they even came to define her nature in later years.

Ballet helped Audrey refine her seamless grace, the most ineffable and yet most powerful aspect of her style. As it is revealed in Audrey's early life, grace was not simply about friendship with a French couturier or a lithe silhouette; like intelligence or imagination, grace comes from within. A profound state of being, her grace was expressed through the subtlest gesture—her posture, voice, even the way she signed her name. However we define grace, Audrey had it in spades, starting with how she moved. As her friend Joe Eula, the renowned fashion illustrator, observed, "She was a dancer, so every move was symphonic. She walked like a dream—*nobody* had that walk."

Audrey's elegance was partially a gift from the gods, but her early ballet lessons, no doubt, helped her glide so magically across a dance floor. In much the same way that Coco Chanel, raised in an orphanage by French nuns, revered the stark simplicity of their black habits, Hepburn never forgot the *pliés* learned in London with Marie Rambert. While Chanel later reworked the nuns' habits into the timeless black Chanel suit we know today, Audrey raised the ability to walk across a room to an art form.

In addition to ballet, Audrey's inner life contributed greatly to why we remain so drawn to her. People who knew Audrey speak of her concentration. Audrey Wilder recalls the "very still center" that Audrey possessed. John Loring, design director of Tiffany's and a friend of later years, noted how

Audrey had the strength of mind to draw her own conclusions about life. "She spoke like she wrote. She thought things through, she spoke slowly, as if the words were being said for the first time, not as if she were saying something she'd said a million times. She was always thinking it through as she went along. It was always *her* opinion, it was not perceived opinion—and by the way, that's what kept her, at all times, modern." Audrey also had an almost Zenlike ability to do one thing at a time. A friend remembers: "When she was at a fitting, she was being fitted. When she was reading a book, she read. When she had her hair done she didn't smoke and eat a tomato sandwich and talk like everyone else. She had enormous focus on what was at hand."

In this respect, Audrey was much like her future costar Fred Astaire, who practiced four hours a day every day of his life. From dance, they both knew how the narrowing of focus can bring great beauty. They also knew that the point was to make art look effortless, its cost in human terms was unimportant. (Amusingly, Humphrey Bogart, Audrey's costar in *Sabrina*, picked up on this aspect of her personality when he said, "She's disciplined, like all those ballet dames.") Along with Coco Chanel, Fred Astaire, Babe Paley, and countless other style setters, Audrey knew that perfection, simplicity, and grace were the ideals. But none of them came by chance; it took supreme concentration, effort, and discipline to turn those ideals into reality.

A perfect example of Audrey's capacity for self-discipline concerns her famous figure. In London, after years of wartime deprivation, Audrey began eating properly again and grew, in her words, "chubby"—at 130 pounds. "I went on an eating binge," she said. "I would eat anything in sight and in any quantity. I'd empty out a jam jar with a spoon. I was crazy about everything I could lay my hands on when the food started appearing. I became quite tubby and put on twenty pounds." Audrey soon decided that at five feet seven, 110 pounds was "the perfect weight" for her. Through sheer will she cut out bread and sweets and lost twenty pounds in a month, and retained virtually the same slim silhouette for the rest of her life.

So, for all of Audrey's vaunted casual elegance, it is naive to think that her outward appearance was a haphazard creation. The first time they met her, both Edith Head and Hubert de Givenchy were struck by Audrey's ability to view herself so analytically. "You have to look at yourself objectively," she advised fans early in her career. "Analyze yourself like an instrument. You have to be absolutely frank with yourself. Face your handicaps, don't try to hide them. Instead, develop something else."

As the tallest girl in her ballet classes, "I tried to make everything an asset," she said of her early years in the corps. "Instead of working on *allegro*—little small tight movements—I took extra courses in *adagio*, so I could use my long lines to my advantage." What Hubert de Givenchy would, in a few years, elevate to haute couture, Audrey learned in an unheated dance studio.

After months of training, Rambert took Audrey aside and told her the difficult truth: "You have wonderful technique, you can always teach, but you will never be a great prima ballerina." Audrey was crushed. Years later, she told her son Sean that she went home that day and just wanted to vanish. Her dream had died. Retelling this, his voice quiets, echoing his mother's pain. "But since she had to work and make a living, she went on to acting, which," Sean says with a faint smile, "didn't turn out so bad."

Audrey scrambled to fill the gap left when the possibility of a career in ballet evaporated. She occasionally modeled for commercial photographers to pick up a few extra shillings, rarely smiling since she was self-conscious about her less than perfect teeth. Perhaps without intending it, this gave her a worldly, mysterious air. She appeared in a print ad for Lacto-Calamine, a beauty lotion, and saw her face in a thousand drugstores. She acquired an agent ("or, rather, an agent acquired me," she said with typical modesty) and began a fledgling career as a chorus girl in slight West End musicals like *High Button Shoes* (1948), *Sauce Tartare* (1949), and *Sauce Piquante* (1950).

In a photo that epitomizes this transitional time in her life, Audrey poses on a rooftop with two other *Sauce Tartare* chorus girls. Surely it is some publicist's setup—the other "girls" are sitting on a block of ice, while Audrey hovers closely in the background. Grinning crookedly, she wears a soft peasant-style dress with cap sleeves. Her hair is mussed in the wind. Her white ballet slippers look impossibly large for her frame. Years away from the self-possessed Givenchy sophisticate, Audrey looks coltish, about twelve years old. Still, there is something in her open face that draws us to her.

A year later, in 1951, Audrey was plucked from the chorus line to utter one sentence, "Who wants a ciggy?" in a British film, *Laughter in Paradise*.

MARCH 1951

ABC Film Review

STORIES AND PICTURES OF THE FILMS COMING YOUR WAY

4D

Audrey Hepburn

ASSOCIATED
BRITISH
ARTISTE

IN THIS ISSUE: DAVID LEWIN WRITES "CLOSE-UPS OF THE STARS I KNOW"
OLIVER LANGLEY INTERVIEWS RICHARD ATTENBOROUGH AND SHEILA SIM

Audrey Hepburn "Roman Holiday" 1953

Edith Head

Whatever *it* was, Hepburn had it. On the strength of this brief appearance as a girl with a vendor's tray, she was offered a seven-year contract with Associated British Films. Audrey didn't sign the contract—she didn't want to be tied to any one studio, particularly one in the United Kingdom, when it seemed all the exciting pictures were being made in America. This proved the right decision, as she was soon spotted by Colette in the lobby of the Hôtel de Paris, and got the lead in the stage production of *Gigi*.

But before Audrey sailed for New York to prepare for her Broadway debut as the young French girl who decided not to become a *grande cocotte*, the London office of Paramount called her agent. There was a part they wanted her to come in and read for: an innocent European princess who escapes her handlers for a night out on the town and meets an American newspaperman, played by Gregory Peck. The film would be directed by William Wyler, shot in sequence in Rome, with costumes by Edith Head. The lineup was complete except for a leading lady—they'd scoured two continents and had yet to find her.

As Audrey recalled, "[My agent] told me a movie was going to be made called *Roman Holiday*. They wanted an unknown, and they were going to test a great many girls. To get the test I had to meet a man named William Wyler. I had no idea who he was. So one day I got an appointment to go to Claridges. I went up to his room wearing my one and only proper dress. I was quite apprehensive. I didn't know what was expected of me. He was very pleasant. He looked me over, and I think I spent five minutes with him."

Audrey's five minutes must have made an impression, since Wyler recommended that she be put under contract—even without seeing her screen test. As he described her: "She impressed me as being very alert, very smart, very talented, very ambitious." But he still had to make sure that her personality translated to the screen before casting her in the lead. Since he couldn't stay to make the test himself, he arranged for British director Thorold Dickinson to shoot it, and left precise instructions on how he wanted it done. As he later explained, "a test is a precarious thing. A good actress might make a very bad test, depending on conditions. You might not get her true personality because of nervousness or whatever. So I asked the director to do an old trick—to continue to run camera and sound after the scene ended, in the hope that the girl would not be aware of it." This would allow them to see Audrey completely relaxed.

When Audrey auditioned at Pinewood Studios outside London for the role of the princess in *Roman Holiday*, she knew little about Hollywood, less about William Wyler, and nothing at all about Edith Head. "Only four years before that I had come out of Holland," she explained. "We hadn't been able to keep up with pictures, so I was way behind." Audrey knew Wyler had come to England searching for an unknown which, as she brightly put it, was her only qualification. "I had no idea who William Wyler was, no sense of what Mr. Wyler could do for my career. I had no sense, period!" she laughed. "I was awfully new, and awfully young, and thrilled just to be going out on auditions and meeting people who seemed to like me." Audrey wasn't thinking in terms of a career as an actress, she merely hoped that if she worked hard and learned her lines, perhaps they might let her have a go at it.

The "little dancer" they'd found in London needn't have worried. Her black and white screen test is charming. As Audrey remembered, "I'd never really acted, never opened my mouth before. There was a young man who read some lines with me. I was so green I didn't really know what to do, and I think Thorold got a little desperate. But he didn't give up, which was what saved the situation. He said, 'Well, we've done this scene now. Why don't you change back into your clothes and then come out and have a chat with me. There are a few things I'd like to know about you.' So I got into my sweater and slacks, and I came back and sat down and talked to him. He asked me a lot of questions about myself, about my work, even about my past during the war in Holland. I suddenly realized, little that I knew, a camera was rolling all the time. My face lit up and then I became very rigid. But that's what made the test. He had me on film being as natural as possible, not trying to act." Although shy and a bit tentative, Audrey's expressive eyes draw us in. She *wants* us to like her. Watching this unknown young girl, we can't help but hang on her every word. Without realizing her full effect, perhaps, she is mesmerizing.

The test reel was sent to Wyler in Rome, who found Audrey irresistible. "She was everything I was looking for," he remembered, "charm, innocence, and talent. She was absolutely enchanting." Paramount agreed and fired off a cable to Richard Mealand, their production chief in London: "Exercise the

option on this lady. The test is certainly one of the best ever made in Hollywood, New York, or London." Audrey was also asked to change her surname to avoid conflict with Katharine Hepburn. She refused. If Paramount wanted her, they would have to take her name too.

Audrey got the part, and forty-six years later, Gregory Peck's voice softens at the memory of that summer in Rome. "Audrey definitely had a good heart, there was nothing mean or petty—it's a character thing. She had a good character, so I think people picked up on that too. She didn't have any of the backstabbing, grasping, petty, gossipy personalities that you see in this business. I liked her a lot; in fact, I loved Audrey. It was easy to love her."

But that was the future. At the time Audrey didn't know how any of it would turn out. Her response to Paramount's decision to cast her as the lead in *Roman Holiday* was humble. First the lead in her first Broadway play, and now this? It was beyond her imagination. When she first came to London, her greatest dream was to put on a tutu and dance at Covent Garden. Now she was packing her bags, preparing for her first-class voyage on the *Queen Mary* to meet the producers of *Gigi* in New York. At the age of twenty-two, she knew her life was about to change, she just didn't know how. "Heaven help me to live up to all of this," she prayed.

audrey and jackie

"Childhood shows the man," wrote Milton, "as morning shows the day." The things Audrey loved as a girl stayed with her her whole life. There was ballet, chocolate (when Arnhem was liberated, Audrey ate all seven chocolate bars given to her by an English soldier and promptly got sick), and, shortly thereafter, cigarettes. "Think about it," observes her friend designer Jeffrey Banks, "what do soldiers give away—Hershey bars and cigarettes! And they're cheap—remember, nobody had any money then."

Interestingly, another style icon, Jacqueline Kennedy Onassis, shared these same pleasures. She was a patron of the American Ballet Theatre, enjoyed a chocolate ice cream cone at Mad Martha's on the Cape, and cupped her cigarette behind her back when photographers took her picture. Beyond youthful fancies, however, there are a startling number of similarities, and a few differences, between the two women.

Born in 1929, Audrey and Jackie were the same age. Both thought they had large feet, although we don't know if Jackie was self-conscious about hers.

Jackie fudged her lineage (in actuality, she was more Irish than French) to impress her in-laws and the American public (those "dentists' wives" as she referred to them in a very un-Audrey note to Oleg Cassini). Audrey was descended from Dutch nobility.

Jackie was consumed with the idea of becoming an actress. In 1956, Gore Vidal thrilled her by taking her to Downey's, an actor's hangout on Eighth Avenue in Manhattan, and introducing her as the "new girl at Warner's." No one recognized the senator's wife—heck, she might have been a dentist's wife for all they knew. Having won an Oscar her first time out with *Roman Holiday*, in 1954, Audrey was not only the new girl at Paramount, she was also, inarguably, the next big thing.

Jackie was an accomplished equestrian. Until November 1993—the last Thanksgiving of her life—she rode to the hounds with the Piedmont Hunt in Upperville, Virginia. Audrey, on the other hand, was thrown from a white stallion during filming of *The Unforgiven*. Newly pregnant, she refused all sedatives and was concerned that her husband, Mel Ferrer, would learn of her fall before she had a chance to tell him herself. In bed for a month, Audrey suffered four broken vertebrae, torn muscles in her lower back, and a badly sprained foot. While recuperating, she responded to over a hundred get well notes and kept a white-leather-framed picture of Diablo, the horse, on her nightstand (along with photos of Mel and his children), telling friends not to blame him for the accident.

Audrey and Jackie both made challenging, shall we say, marriages to men who were charismatic, self-centered, and, perhaps without intending it, at times cruel. In the rough pace of the world, both women were sometimes an afterthought in their husbands' realms. After two marriages, both found love—but not marriage—with sympathetic men who adored them. They each had two children, would have had more if it were possible, and considered being a mother their highest calling. "If you bungle raising your children," said Jackie, "I don't think whatever else you do matters."

According to Polly Mellen, creative director of *Allure* magazine, there were distinct similarities between Audrey's and Jackie's style—"they dressed in an eliminated way—not garish or glitter! It was the most refined WASP way of dressing." Fashionwise, Audrey and Jackie followed a similar arc: proper French suits for public events, turtleneck and slacks during off hours. They both discovered Valentino around the same time (Jackie wore a cream-colored lace Valentino dress when she married Aristotle Onassis in 1968), and at the end of their lives, losing none of their style, favored everyday khakis, T-shirts, and flats.

Jackie grew up to become First Lady (a title she hated because she thought it made her sound like a racehorse) and later, when history intervened, a legend. So did Audrey.

She was the first to

make something
that's not sexy, sexy.

CYNTHIA ROWLEY

"I have no time to shop for 'Audrey'
clothes. I have two dinner dresses and slacks,
and horrible gaps in between."

— A H

woman of the year

"AUDREY CAME TO TOWN," recalls Audrey Wilder, "and everyone immediately wanted to lose ten pounds." The town was Hollywood and Audrey had just won the Academy Award for Best Actress for her portrayal of Princess Anne in *Roman Holiday*, her first appearance in a major motion picture. To moviegoers who were meeting this gamine beauty, her onscreen presence was electrifying. Ralph Lauren admits that "in every movie I have ever watched, starting with *Roman Holiday*, I was in love with Audrey Hepburn. I played every part—I was Gregory Peck a long time ago! I was Bill Holden, I was Cary Grant, I was her biggest fan."

Just as Audrey's ability to connect with an audience was instantaneous, her effect on fashion was immediate. As the *New York Times* observed, "Thanks to their first glimpse of Audrey Hepburn in *Roman Holiday*, half a generation of young females stopped stuffing their bras and teetering on stiletto heels." In the film, Princess Anne moves anonymously among the masses dressed like a Vassar girl circa 1952. Wearing a full skirt cinched at the waist with a thick belt, a cotton button-down shirt with the sleeves rolled up and a silk kerchief around her neck, she could be any well-bred sophomore seeing *Roma* for the first time. Yet, as simple as her style appears, Audrey ushered in a modern look that spoke to millions of women. Working in collaboration with Edith Head, she developed a sophisticated wardrobe that aspiring young women could emulate.

In the moving final scene of *Roman Holiday*, the princess is asked by a reporter which city she would most remember from her trip. The room goes silent, waiting for her response.

"Rome," she answers finally, rounding her "O" and looking Gregory Peck square in the eye. A European city never sounded so ravishing, so full of love and memory and lost possibility. "Rome." She might also have said, in all honesty, "Ferragamo." For Rome was where Audrey discovered Italian shoemaker Salvatore Ferragamo, of whom she remained a loyal customer for the rest of her life, wearing his heels as a young starlet and his blue and white driving moccasins in her sixties.

It was not surprising that Audrey should find her way to Ferragamo — who counted most of the well-dressed women of the mid–twentieth century as his clients, and fans, including Sophia Loren, Greta Garbo, the Duchess of Windsor, Claire Boothe Luce, Ava Gardner, and Lauren Bacall. Shoes were the dapper Ferragamo's obsession, and he labored to produce the exquisitely crafted, glamorous yet comfortable shoes Italians were renowned for.

There was plenty of time for shopping jaunts during this production, since *Roman Holiday* was a leisurely six-month shoot. "Wyler liked to take his time," Gregory Peck remembers. "We worked out each scene until we felt comfortable with it. There was no hustle." *Roman Holiday* was a special experience for everyone who worked on the set. "For six months," confides Peck, "we believed in that fairy story — that she was a princess and I was the newspaperman. I think we just started believing it, Audrey and I, and the director too — the funny scenes were funny to us, and the sad scenes were quite tragic."

During the shooting Audrey had no idea how the picture would be received, but more experienced actors knew what was in store for her. A few weeks into production, Gregory Peck asked his agent what the billing on the picture was and he said: "Gregory Peck in *Roman Holiday*." Peck said, "You can't do that — she's got to have equal billing. It's not the newspaperman's story, it's the princess's story." When told that it was very generous of him to give an unknown equal billing, Peck laughs and says, "I think it was pragmatic of me." Hollywood agreed with his assessment. Once *Roman Holiday* hit the screens, the offers poured in for Audrey, and she never struggled for work again. In quick succession Audrey made *Sabrina* with Humphrey Bogart and

William Holden, *Funny Face* with Fred Astaire, and *Love in the Afternoon* with Gary Cooper. Her fashion influence continued unabated in each of these films that followed her first appearance in full skirt and flat shoes.

AUDREY'S EXHILARATING influence on fashion is a remarkable joyride that did not begin and end in 1953 but continues to this day. In fact, three decades after the film's American debut, Gregory Peck and his wife traveled to Beijing to celebrate the release of *Roman Holiday* in China. "When we climbed out of the airplane," Peck remembers, "I saw forty Chinese girls dressed like the princess in *Roman Holiday*! They had the bangs, they had the Audrey hairdo, with the skirts that fell between the knees and the ankle, and the pleated blouses—I think they expected to see the young Gregory Peck, and here comes this fellow who's got some gray hair and a little creaky in the joints!" Peck believes Audrey had such an impact on fashion because she possessed "both style and substance. She brought something new to the screen. Her European upbringing. She had a Dutch mother and an English father. You have to remember she experienced the war under the Nazis, so she wasn't the typical American. So she brought her experiences to her sense of style, and that difference was appealing."

Some critics have suggested that Audrey's influence on fashion was simply a matter of good timing: She appeared at the onset of the 1950s, when society was ready to broaden the "acceptable" standards of beauty. Other fashion commentators believed her popularity rose in sync with the Eisenhower era, a time of peace and prosperity, but time has shown that Audrey's stylish effect relied most upon her ageless appeal. Part of Audrey's attraction, of course, is that she was not the breezy California girl next door. Her black turtleneck, leggings, ballet flats, and gamine haircut, even the yappy dog that went with her everywhere, were *very* European. Introduced to American moviegoers as Princess Anne, Audrey Hepburn offered an exotic—and less blatantly sexy—antidote to the blowsy blondes like Marilyn Monroe and Jayne Mansfield that Hollywood was serving up at the time. Her close friend and fellow actor, Roger Moore, once remarked, "Audrey gave beauty a new concept. Movie stars in the fifties looked like Lana Turner and Ava Gardner. Then along came this waiflike creature with these doe eyes. But what made her different was her honesty, sincerity, and sense of fun."

Audrey Wilder, Billy's wife, became a close friend of Audrey's when he directed her in *Sabrina* and later, when she lived in Hollywood. Like Hepburn, she has a reverence for clothing—to this day she can discuss the subtleties of Karl Lagerfeld's career with the precision of any *Vogue* editor, believes a woman should *always* dress, even if she is just going to the supermarket, and with the verve and generosity one expects from a Billy Wilder character, is capable of passing along a Chanel suit to Jennifer Grant, Cary Grant and Dyan Cannon's daughter, because "she's a kid! It looks better on her than it does me—I don't know *what* I was thinking when I bought it!"

Audrey Wilder has rare insight into Audrey's offscreen style. "Audrey had a big effect on fashion generally, and she rarely skimped on quality. If she wore a shirt, it was a good shirt, a first-class shirt! Or a first-class hat! But simple—I mean, if she was gardening, or cooking, or something like that." The two Audreys used to shop at a store on Wilshire Boulevard called Jax, cattycorner to the Beverly Wilshire Hotel. If Hepburn wasn't getting gussied up, she liked practical clothing. "The store sold velveteen pantsuits. Audrey loved them!" remembers Mrs. Wilder. "She bought a lot of them and they were cheap—jackets, $60, pants, $40. They came in every color—black, velveteen brown, pink, green, blue, and you could mix them, she loved that, and she bought a lot of them. Everybody that came from Europe, they loved the stuff! And they looked good in it! Simple, three or four buttons, with a nice little pocket. Everybody bought them, they were flying off the hangers!"

Photographer Bob Willoughby, who shot Audrey Hepburn as well as practically every other star of the era, has different memories of Jax. "As for the place being reasonably priced—no way! It was very upmarket for the times. The salesgirls were generally barefoot, and rarely even noticed the customers. They stood in the back and ignored anyone they didn't know or who wasn't famous." Willoughby believes he got good service only because he had used them for a couple of fashion jobs for *Life*, and knew Jack and Sally Hansen, the owners.

LIKE RALPH LAUREN, designer Cynthia Rowley first saw Audrey in *Roman Holiday* (on television in the early 1970s) and immediately felt a connection with her. "I would look at some of the other stars like Sophia

Loren and Marilyn Monroe, and I would think—there's just no way, I could never be like them. That was a man's idea of beauty, and Audrey was more like a woman's idea of beauty. It was something that was attainable, that I could identify with."

Audrey's allure had little in common with the sweater girls of the day. Billy Wilder, who directed and produced *Sabrina*, picked up on her sophisticated appeal, saying, "This girl, single-handedly, may make bosoms a thing of the past." Wilder also understood that Audrey's effect on audiences went beyond fashion. "She drew them in. She could say something risqué, but the way she did it had a kind of elegance that you could not, under any circumstance, mistake."

While there was definitely a sexual element to Audrey's appeal, hers was a subtle, grown-up kind of sexuality for a newly style-conscious America that would, in a few short years, embrace the heady optimism of Camelot, the Kennedys, and the 1960s. "Sex appeal is something that you feel deep down inside. It's suggested rather than shown," Audrey mused. "I'm not as well-stacked as Sophia Loren or Gina Lollobrigida, but there is more to sex appeal than just measurements. I don't need a bedroom to prove my womanliness. I can convey just as much appeal fully clothed, picking apples off a tree or standing in the rain." As Cynthia Rowley put it: "Audrey was the first to make something that's not sexy, sexy."

The struggling ballet student of a few years before was growing up, becoming more mature and confident as the weeks passed. The transformation was fascinating, and it was with good reason that Audrey became an "overnight success." Her ascent was extraordinary, and no less remarkable because, like all great Cinderella stories, she seemed to come from nowhere. Director Stanley Donen, who would go on to direct Audrey in *Funny Face*, *Charade*, and *Two for the Road*, shares this sentiment: "The first time I saw Audrey Hepburn was in *Roman Holiday*. There have only been a few firsts in my life that have rattled me so much—the first time I saw Fred Astaire, the first time I saw Marlon Brando. It was obvious to me that she was going to join a group into which a few artists are admitted: Chaplin, Astaire, Brando."

Henry Luce had the same visceral response to Audrey. On September 7, 1953, Audrey was on the cover of *Time* magazine, the first time the editors so

honored an unknown star of a newly released film. That same year, *Life* named her Woman of the Year. "What makes Audrey's charm?" the magazine headlined. The answer: "Audrey defies definition. She is both waif and woman of the world. She is disarmingly friendly and strangely aloof." Audrey held mystery behind her hazel eyes, whereas other movie stars blared the obvious; clearly, she had lived a life.

And the life she was living was about to get more interesting, when Hepburn met actor Mel Ferrer at the London premiere of *Roman Holiday* in July 1953. Ferrer was a close friend of Gregory Peck's from the La Jolla Playhouse, which they founded in 1947 to give stars like Patricia Neal, Vincent Price, Dorothy McGuire, Jane Wyatt, and Constance Collier stage work during the summer. Peck was in London shooting *Night People*, while Ferrer was shooting MGM's *Knights of the Round Table* at Pinewood Studios, and Peck suggested Mel come to the party Audrey's mother was hosting at her flat in Mayfair.

Cecil Beaton was at the same party, and in his diary recorded that Mel Ferrer was "a charming, gangling man, [who] described A.H. to me as 'the biggest thing to come down the turnpike.'" Audrey must have felt similarly well disposed toward Mel, in spite of the fact that he was twice divorced, the father of four, and twelve years her senior, because when he called shortly thereafter (at Peck's suggestion), they quickly got together. A man of vivid imagination, talent, and tenacity, Mel immediately sensed that Audrey was special. And he did not intend to let her slip away.

In tall, confident, charismatic Mel, Audrey thought she had found her knight-errant. To others, he seemed more like a kingly error. Listed in the Social Register, Melchior Gaston Ferrer was one of those men who went to Princeton and never let you forget it—a real standout in a town where most of the studio heads were former furriers with a third-grade education. A producer, director, and an actor—a triple threat—he also had the reputation of a guy with a major attitude.

At the time, Rosemary Clooney and Audrey were young starlets on the Paramount lot together. Clooney was working on *White Christmas*, while Audrey was shooting *Sabrina*. With neighboring dressing rooms, they became friends.

"I was married to José Ferrer at the time—no relation to Mel," Clooney recalls, "and one night I invited Audrey home for dinner. It was just the two of us, and after dinner we were sitting, watching television, I think, and she asked me, 'What do you think of Mel Ferrer?' And I said: 'Oh, my God, he's *the worst*—he'd walk over anyone who got in his way, he steamrolls women to get what he wants, he's terrible!'

"She didn't say much, just, 'Hmmmmm.'

"Later, after she'd left, I spoke to José and said, 'I think I said something that maybe I shouldn't have—'

"And he said, 'What's that?'

"And I said, 'She asked what I thought of Mel, and I told her.'

"José said, 'Big mistake.'

"'Why?'

"'She's dating him!'"

Audrey and Rosie later joked about it and Audrey eventually forgave her. In fact, Mel and Audrey rented the Ferrers' weekend house in Pound Ridge when they appeared in *Ondine* on Broadway from February through June 1954.

All the while, and in spite of her mother's objections, the relationship between Mel and Audrey deepened. They lived together in the Village while they starred together on Broadway in *Ondine*, the story of a water sprite and the knight who cannot be faithful to her, where Mel introduced Audrey to jazz and New York nightlife. They were both Noel Coward fans. For his thirty-seventh birthday in August, Audrey gave Mel a platinum Rolex watch engraved with the Coward title "Mad About the Boy."

After *Ondine*'s run, which earned Audrey a Tony Award for best female actress, they married in Switzerland on September 24, 1954. Audrey, who had, perhaps, the fear of the era that no man would ever ask her to marry, was blissfully happy. "Like many teenagers," she later admitted, "I thought I was such an ugly thing that no one would ever want me for a wife. . . . Which is why I always say to Mel, 'Thanks to you, I'm off the shelf!'" For her wedding day, Audrey wore a white Pierre Balmain dress, a delicate crown of white roses in her hair, and white gloves. The new Mr. and Mrs. Ferrer honeymooned in Albano, Italy, about twenty miles outside Rome, and Mel remembered the carloads of paparazzi and journalists who followed their every move—they even had to establish a cordon of security around the country farmhouse he had rented to give themselves some peace.

THREE YEARS AFTER their marriage came *Funny Face*, in 1957, the Stanley Donen confection that made more designers decide to become designers than perhaps any other film. Jeffrey Banks first saw it in Washington, D.C., at the age of eleven. It was paired with *Lili*, the Leslie Caron movie (featuring Mel Ferrer) as a double feature at the Circle Theater, a revival house on M Street in Georgetown. Jeffrey dragged his mother and made her sit through both movies twice. "From that moment," he remembers, "I was hooked on Audrey and becoming a designer!"

Fresh out of the Parsons School of Design in New York, young Isaac Mizrahi approached Jeffrey Banks for a job. He was so talented that Jeffrey took one look at Isaac's sketchbook, hired him on the spot, and knew he'd be lucky if he stayed a year. One day they were talking in the studio and *Funny Face* came up. Isaac confessed that he had never seen it. "How can you call yourself a designer when you've never seen *Funny Face*?" Jeffrey exclaimed. The boy was a near prodigy, but he still had a thing or two to learn. Jeffrey immediately went out and bought him a copy. Mizrahi, for his part, loved *Funny Face* and cited Audrey as a major influence in his vision of classic American sportswear. In fact, Mizrahi went on to become one of the most beloved designers of his generation before shifting his attention to films and Hollywood.

As a teenager in Phoenix, Arizona, Steven Spielberg, who would direct Audrey in her final motion picture, *Always*, was dragged kicking and screaming by his parents to see *Funny Face* at the drive-in. The moment he saw Audrey, Steven was mesmerized. Such a glamorous world they lived in! That night he fell in love with Audrey, and as she looked into the camera, out into the audience, he felt in some way she was loving him back. Audrey's gift as an actress was that looking at her, millions of people around the world felt the same way Spielberg did.

A romance starring Fred Astaire, set mostly in Paris against the backdrop of haute couture, *Funny Face* seemed tailor made for Audrey. At first her agent, Kurt Frings, angrily turned it down, deeming the "trivial musical" too inconsequential for a star of Audrey's magnitude. But after the script was sent to Audrey at the Raphaël in Paris, she read it in two hours. "I read it in Paris," remembered Hepburn, "and I fell in love with it. It was a charming story, plus I knew that I would get to dance with Fred Astaire." The part was so close to

Audrey that even her mother told screenwriter Leonard Gershe she could not believe it was written by someone who didn't know her daughter.

There was only one minor problem in this whole brilliant scenario: Edith Head was once again assigned to the picture and, as Stanley Donen put it, "How could Edith Head possibly work on a fashion picture?" Audrey and Donen quickly agreed that Givenchy was the only choice, and relegated Head to create Kay Thompson's wardrobe. Knowing a good deal about fashion herself, Thompson—who would go on to write the *Eloise* series, about the little girl who lives at the Plaza Hotel—was not pleased.

Once the wardrobe situation was settled, one could see that the baroness was right. In many ways, *Funny Face* is an almost uncanny metaphor for Audrey's emerging style and stardom. In the film, Jo Stockton, a downtown bohemian bookworm, is "discovered" by a Diana Vreeland–type magazine editor (played by Kay Thompson) and a charming fashion photographer, with the debonair Fred Astaire filling the fictional shoes of Richard Avedon. While in Paris under their tutelage, Jo Stockton is transformed into a confident cover girl. When the curtain rises at the salon show, Audrey emerges, holding her head as regally as an Egyptian princess, in a flawless Givenchy creation the color of dawn. The audience's applause washes over her in waves of love. We catch our breath at the sight of her. Such is the power of fashion and film. And Audrey.

We need think only of the photographs Richard Avedon took of Hepburn for this film to see her vital influence on fashion: In a slim-waisted black dress she holds a bouquet of balloons in front of the Louvre, as if she herself might fly away at any moment; dressed in a bouclé wool travel suit, carrying her lapdog Famous and a chic rattan traveling case, she stands by a train, surrounded by smoke and mystery. Even slumming with Fred Astaire in smoky bars, with a cropped A-line raincoat tossed over her black Greenwich Village ensemble, Audrey looks fabulous.

Fred Astaire's character, Dick Avery, was based on Richard Avedon and in many ways, save for the ugly-duckling part, *Funny Face* mirrored Audrey's early experiences posing for him. "The first thing I saw when I came to America thirty-six years ago was the Statue of Liberty," Audrey recalled, presenting Avedon with a Council of Fashion Designers of America (CFDA) Lifetime Achievement Award in 1989. "The second—Richard Avedon. Before

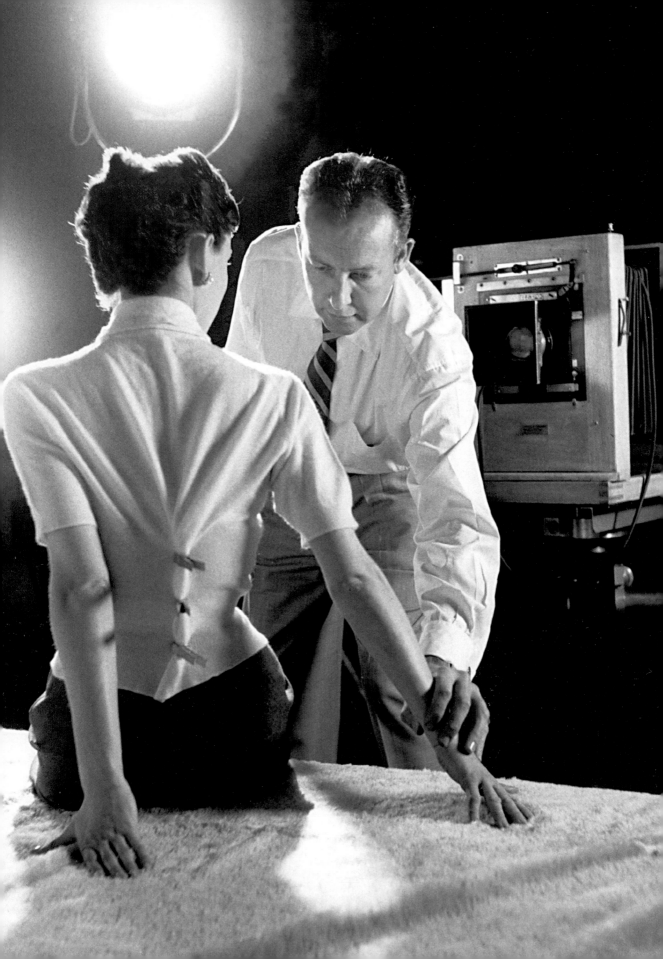

I knew it I was in front of Richard Avedon's camera, lights flashing, music going, Richard snapping away a mile a minute, dashing from one angle to the other like a hummingbird. . . . For Richard, I have happily swung from swings, stood in clouds of steam, been drenched in rain, and descended endless flights of stairs without looking and without breaking my neck."

Polly Mellen, then Diana Vreeland's young fashion assistant, was on one of those early shoots for *Harper's Bazaar* with Richard and Audrey. "She was charming, just charming, no problems about wanting to wear one dress or another. . . . And Dick Avedon just woos, that's his way and especially with Audrey—he just sits her down with tea or coffee and just *woos*." There were no star trips working with Audrey. "We were about the same age and she was just charming," recalls Mellen, "with beautiful manners. But we were all brought up like that then, we had to be. We were raised that way, it was a different milieu, when graciousness and manners *mattered*."

As Audrey gained confidence, she realized that the photographers she posed for, like the directors, costumers, and makeup men, were her collaborators. She worked with them to present her best self to the public. Bob Willoughby was one of the first photographers to shoot Audrey when she arrived in Hollywood. One day in 1953 he got a call from his agent, who sent him to Paramount to shoot a new starlet who'd just made a film in Rome with Greg Peck. Word on the street was that it was pretty good.

"So I went over," Bob remembers, "and she was very special—the usual Hollywood starlet, this wasn't. I was very impressed with Audrey, but *everybody* there was taken with her. If you're used to crew members, and makeup people, and wardrobe, then you'd know they reacted differently to her than to the usual starlet. She had something that they all had antennas up for. Audrey comes in, and you don't forget her.

"I think, in retrospect, it was that Audrey was such a lady herself. You knew she wasn't a real princess, but you still gave her deferential treatment. She had class that the average young American girl never had. And, you know, she never changed all her life. All the years that I knew her and worked with her. Wherever she was, in Europe or America, people respected her. I can't think of anybody else that I have worked with that would have such devotion from her friends."

Did Audrey have a lot of creative input into the photos? Willoughby says that Audrey trusted him—and once he gained her trust, she would do anything for him. "Audrey had approval of all her stills and she would go through them. So she saw the kind of pictures I was taking. There was a great rapport that Audrey and I had. It was just a nod of the head. She didn't have to say anything to me, I could sense what was happening."

Sid Avery, another Hollywood photographer who shot Audrey at the beginning of her career, said that "Audrey had her own concepts of how she should look and how she should work. It was never imposed in a strong way, but I knew that when she made a suggestion, there was a lot of thought and quality behind it.

"I always felt that I was shooting my daughter, someone who had been around me a lot. There always was a great comfort in being with her," he remembers over forty years after first meeting Audrey. "You never got a feeling that you're interrupting, or you shouldn't be doing what you're doing.

"Audrey was so impish and yet so simply beautiful. A lot of the other celebrities depended on other things, physically—on their breasts and their shape. She didn't make a big thing out of that, and for that reason, I thought she was wonderful. Because you didn't have to be conscious of the physique, you were only conscious of the persona."

Bob Willoughby, too, feels that Audrey's persona drew people to her as much as her beauty. "Her character, like most people's—you don't learn that. That's something that you have when you're born. And she just was unique! There are people like Bill Holden, or Jack Lemmon—these are people that I really enjoyed working with. They would be the only kind of people that I would bring back home for dinner tonight! Ninety-nine percent of the people in Hollywood I wouldn't even consider bringing into my home, but Audrey, yes."

IN CREATING HER distinctive visual imprint with Givenchy, as well as the directors and the photographers she worked with, the self-discipline Audrey developed during her years as an aspiring ballerina served her well. She instinctively knew what suited her and rigorously discarded what didn't "work." Just as Joan Crawford wore broad shoulders to balance her wide hips, Hepburn exploited her strong points to maximum advantage. Instead of hiding

the fact that she was, in her own words, "just a skinny broad," she worked with Givenchy to develop an image that *emphasized* her thinness, height, and singularly linear form. In the same way that she culled her photographs for those that conveyed her best image, she took what others might consider flaws and brought them to the forefront, wearing black and solid colors as well as cinched waists and narrow-cut trousers that drew attention to her delicate proportions. She was so successful in countering contemporary notions of beauty that *Vogue* hailed her as "today's wonder girl," who "has so captured the public imagination and the mood of the time that she established a new standard of beauty, and every other face now approximates the 'Hepburn look.'"

But in spite of her well-bred personality, Audrey held very strong opinions about what she would and would not wear, as seen in her decision to use Givenchy instead of Edith Head in *Sabrina*. Having studied her flaws and attributes, she developed rules about her personal style and stuck with them. In fact, she had a memorable—and rare—tiff with Stanley Donen during the filming of *Funny Face*, when he flew in the face of what she considered reason. As Donen remembers, "Audrey and I agreed she would wear black, tight-fitting pants, a black sweater, and black shoes. I wanted her to wear white socks with it and she was stunned. 'Absolutely not!' she said. 'It will spoil the whole black silhouette and cut the line at my feet!' I said, 'If you don't wear the white socks, you will fade into the background, there will be no definition to your movement, and the dance sequence will be bland and dull.' She burst into tears and ran into her dressing room. After a little while she regained her composure, put on the white socks, returned to the set, and went ahead without a whimper.

"Later," Donen added, "when she saw the sequence, she sent me a note saying, 'You were right about the socks. Love, Audrey.'"

Audrey, for her part, said that she did *not* cry over the white socks. "I don't remember being quite that emotional about it," she said. "But Stanley obviously understood how much I cared about how I looked, because I am rather complex. But what I did not tell Stanley until years later was that there was something he did not realize at the time about why I was so upset. You see, as a little girl I had a terrible complex about my big feet—I wear eight and a half—and I'd grown up with ballerinas who were little things. I was always too tall, and if I wore white socks, people were going to see what big feet I had, compared to the girls I always admired with pretty little feet and pretty shoulders and a bosom and everything I didn't have."

IN ADDITION TO the high-fashion story line, there were reasons why the baroness could not believe *Funny Face* was written by someone who did not know her daughter. Like Jo Stockton, Hepburn also saw herself as an unlikely fashion model. Both the character and the actress were beguiling combinations of intelligence and modesty, composure and flightiness, confidence and vulnerability. It was Audrey's ability to contain these opposites within her, as well as her capacity to face her fear and shyness and work through them, that may be another reason we find her so compelling.

It may be no accident that Hepburn heroines often undergo transformations—from the wearied princess who discovers the magic of Rome and the lovelorn chauffeur's daughter who becomes a Paris sophisticate to the young cellist who finds *l'objet d'amour* in the afternoon and the common cockney girl who passes as a princess at the ball. Audrey played these women so well because she knew their uncertainty, hope, and yearning for beauty.

Like her *Funny Face* character, Audrey retained an authentic modesty throughout her career in spite of her early rise to fame—an uncommon and compelling trait. This quality makes us feel close to her; more than any other movie actress, she was a star who seemed within our reach. As a reporter once wrote, "Audrey Hepburn looks like every girl and like no girl." She could rattle off her flaws as quickly as most actresses offered their measurements, but, as cameraman Franz Planer once said of her, "She has lots of faults that make her Audrey Hepburn. Thick eyebrows, uneven teeth. She doesn't mind if her hair is disheveled or if she falls into a pot of soup. She is a real girl."

Hepburn had the discipline and the talent necessary to become a world-famous actress, but she also had the rare ability not to take herself *too* seriously—both on and off the screen. Gregory Peck always considered Audrey's sense of humor one of her most undervalued assets. "She was a cutup, she was a clown," he says, "I think that would surprise people who didn't know her. She could always make me laugh between scenes. I think maybe she didn't have enough roles where she could be a cutup. I think producers saw her and only put her in these serious roles—she was a comic."

Audrey recalled one funny instance, of many, that occurred during the filming of *Funny Face*. "We had a running gag, using Anglo-Franco terms in the wrong way. For example, when the light would come on in airplanes and alert us to stop smoking, it would read *Ne pas fumer*. That's when we'd all look at each other and say, 'It's time to stop fuming.' In spite of her grace and beauty, Audrey was approachable, with a down-to-earth sense of humor. "Audrey always looked regal," says designer Michael Kors, "but she also displayed a wonderful offhand attitude. She always seemed comfortable in her clothes." Audrey was at ease with herself, she made a point of making others feel at ease, and this quality came through onscreen. As Givenchy said, "Audrey knew herself perfectly—the qualities as well as the flaws she perceived herself as having."

Another *Funny Face* anecdote reveals much about Hepburn's ability to take herself seriously—but not too seriously. The last scene in the movie is flawless, much like its two stars: The impossibly elegant Audrey Hepburn and Fred Astaire, reunited at last, dance away on a barge floating down the river. Dressed in a mid-length pure white wedding dress with a neckline and cap sleeves echoed by designer Vera Wang, Audrey is eloquent as she and Astaire sing the Gershwin tune "S'Wonderful," drifting toward the sunset. But like so much in the movies—and in life—the story behind the scenes was much less glamorous than the glossy perfection we see onscreen. As director Stanley Donen recalled, "It had been raining for weeks and weeks, but finally we went out to shoot on this little island which was not much more than a strip of grass between two streams. Everyone was tense until Audrey suddenly quipped, 'Here I've been waiting twenty years to dance with Fred Astaire and what do I get? Mud in my eye!'"

Years later Audrey told her own story, perhaps only a bit out of school, about Donen and this same scene. "Stanley, who at the time was perfecting his French, was photographing Fred and me floating down a stream on a little raft at the end of the picture. Stanley wanted to dress up the scene by having us followed by a flock of swans as the picture faded out—only the swan wrangler, as we called him, was late with his cue. And so, with the camera rolling, a desperately frantic Stanley started yelling at the top of his lungs, '*Les singes! Les singes!*'

"What he meant to say," Audrey remembered, laughing, "was '*Les cygnes!*' or swans. Instead, he was calling out for monkeys."

Audrey's irrepressible personality was as much a part of her style, and her appeal, as ballet slippers and oversized sunglasses. Alongside Audrey's beauty, which was considerable, it was really the other facets of her personality—such as her modesty, generosity, and even occasional insecurity—that made audiences root for her.

By the time *Funny Face* and *Love in the Afternoon* were released in 1957, Audrey was so linked to a certain kind of style that her first name became an adjective, synonymous with a well-bred, sophisticated, American look. "That's *so* Audrey!" became the mantra for well-dressed women—a shorthand that is still seen today in the work of Bill Blass, Ralph Lauren, Michael Kors, Oscar de la Renta, and Cynthia Rowley.

In 1991, at the Lincoln Center Film Society's Salute to Audrey Hepburn, Ralph Lauren brought down the house when he spoke of Audrey's extraordinary influence on fashion. "As a fashion designer," he told the crowd, "I can tell you, Audrey Hepburn's name is mentioned probably every minute—by every magazine editor or fashion assistant. And the way they mention it, they say, 'Oh, that's very Audrey!'" The audience roared. Ralph smiled shyly, giving Audrey a sidelong glance. "I don't know if Audrey has ever heard that, but maybe Givenchy has."

Audrey clapped her hands together and laughed at Ralph, her great friend. Although she had just a glimmering of how much the world loved her, she did know a thing or two about being "Audrey."

famous **famous**

"Who thinks you're as
fantastic as your dog?"

— A H

Famous, a yappy, high-strung Yorkie, was
Audrey's most, well, *famous* dog. "She
was gaga over that dog," remembers Billy
Wilder. "She was ga-ga over all the dogs
she had, and she always had one." A gift
from Mel in 1956, Famous made a cameo
appearance in *Funny Face*, lounged in his
owner's lap between takes in *Breakfast at
Tiffany's*, and appeared in countless Avedon
shoots. In the Freud-happy fifties, one director saw Famous as a "child substitute" for
Audrey—she doted on him, took him everywhere, and overlooked his many faults. In
this respect Famous may have been more
of a warmup for life with her husbands
than with her children.

Unfortunately, Famous, gleaning
nothing from his famously well-behaved
owner, was not a well-behaved dog. Once,
Audrey took him to visit Audrey and Billy
Wilder's home in Los Angeles. "Famous is
absolutely perfectly well behaved," Audrey
assured her hostess. A teacup-sized terror,
he took one look at the Wilders' Yorkie,
Fifty, and peed on all of their silk Louis XIV
living room chairs. Hepburn was mortified,
while Audrey Wilder found it hilarious.

In spite of his Brando-esque antics, "Famey," as he was known to Audrey and her girlfriends, could never get into *real* trouble. And Famous knew that. After all, he was a professional, he did his job, which was keeping Audrey happy. And like so many Hollywood stars whose sins are eternally forgiven, he photographed well, which always helps when you're in a tight spot with Billy Wilder. When the cameras rolled, Hollywood knew that Famous (like Audrey) delivered the goods. But Audrey's dog began exhibiting some *very* unstarlike behavior. Maybe the stress of public life was too much for him. Perhaps all the attention had gone to his tiny beribboned head. In some danger of becoming the Judy Garland of the canine set, Famous was prescribed tranquilizers to calm him down.

In 1958 Audrey one-upped dog lovers

everywhere and adopted a fawn in preparation for *Green Mansions*. With its huge brown eyes and skinny legs, everyone agreed the deer looked just like its owner. Needless to say, Famey was not happy. In fact, Famey was fuming. He hid behind lamps, angry when Ip was fed and he wasn't. "You have to understand," said photographer Bob Willoughby, "Famous *adored* Audrey."

Audrey fed Ip from a baby bottle every two hours. "For two and a half months it lived in our house," said Mel. "It ate its bowl of Pablum with us in the dining room and at night it slept in our bathroom." Ip followed Audrey around the supermarket— imagine coming across those two coltish creatures in the produce aisle. On their private Christmas card that year, Ip and Famous (who must have called a temporary détente) are posed on the couch between Mel and Audrey. Everyone is all smiles.

During filming of *The Children's Hour* in 1960, Mel and Audrey rented a house on Sunset Boulevard. "We called it 'The Boulevard of Broken Dreams,'" Audrey Wilder recalls brightly, "for divorcées and women between engagements." It didn't help Audrey's already-muted opinion of Hollywood when Famous ran away from home and was hit by a car, dying in her arms. Heartbroken, Audrey took her son Sean with her to Paris, where Mel was filming *The Longest Day*. Sizing up the situation like a good husband, Mel bought Audrey another Yorkie named Assam of Assam. He looked a lot like Famous. In time, Audrey grew to love him too.

For all her vaunted love for animals, Audrey was not a cat person. At a *Harper's*

Bazaar shoot in Paris the next spring, a white cat was brought along for atmosphere (along with Mel, Dick Avedon, Buster Keaton, Art Buchwald, and a pile of hard-sided Vuitton luggage). Art director Henry Wolf remembers: "That cat scratched Audrey and we couldn't shoot one side of her face for a few days. . . . I think someone forgot to feed it."

Audrey eventually graduated from Yorkies and a deer to Jack Russell terriers, those rowdy, shoebox-sized dogs that think they're German shepherds. At one time she had five, among them, Tupper, a gift from Audrey to Robert Wolders, Rob, for his fiftieth birthday. "Robbie had never had a dog of his own, and I thought he should have one," she said, perhaps remembering the joy Famous brought her. And although Missy and Tupper, the two remaining dogs, got along fine when she was alive, they had to be separated after her death—the magic was over, for their relationship with Audrey was no longer at its center.

"I think an animal, especially a dog, is possibly the purest experience you can have," Audrey once opined. "No person, and few children . . . are as unpremeditated, as undemanding, really. They only ask to survive. They want to eat. They are totally dependent on you, and therefore completely vulnerable. And this complete vulnerability is what enables you to open up your heart completely, which you rarely do to a human being."

Now, honestly, what are a few ruined chairs compared to all that?

Audrey had an angelic
She didn't
than everyone, she just
an energy, a sort
within her that

quality about her.
act like she was better
had a presence,
of light coming from
was overwhelming.

KEVYN AUCOIN

that funny face

IT IS SIX O'CLOCK in the evening at suite fourteen at the Ritz hotel
in Paris, the classic time for "cinq-à-sept," when the Frenchman sees his mistress. In the role of Ariane, a cello student posing as a young woman of certain
ways, Audrey Hepburn crawls across the floor with only one shoe, wearing a
white Givenchy dress with fitted bodice and full skirt, embroidered with a
scattering of flowers. It is the perfect dress for a love affair in the afternoon
with Frank Flannagan, the womanizing entrepreneur played by Gary Cooper.

"I can't show up in just one shoe," Ariane laments, late for her next
invented rendezvous.

"Why not? You have a very handsome foot," Flannagan parries, the
missing shoe in the pocket of his smoking jacket.

"It's too big," Ariane protests as she searches beneath the telephone
table.

"It's perfect. As a matter of fact, everything about you is perfect,"
Flannagan says, crawling beside her.

"I'm too thin and my ears stick out, my teeth are crooked and my neck's
much too long."

"Maybe so, but I love the way it all hangs together. It's that Parisian
thing you've got, that certain *quelque chose*, as they say on the Left Bank."

Frank Flannagan was right—there was an indefinable quality to Audrey

Hepburn's beauty, a quality that even the suavest leading man was hard pressed to put into words. It was something that the greatest directors could not fully capture, nor was it fully portrayed in any of the thousands of photographs taken during her lifetime. Audrey's beauty lay well below the surface of her flawless skin; it was more in her expression than in any one physical attribute. For this reason, Richard Avedon said, "I have always found her impossible to photograph. She has achieved in herself the ultimate portrait."

However she was portrayed, and whomever she was portraying, the effect of Audrey Hepburn's physical appearance was startling. One look at Audrey as most people first saw her, as Princess Anne in *Roman Holiday*, and we cannot help but notice her luminous, wide-set eyes, her arched brows and thick lashes, her classic bone structure. But it is the clear, open gaze with which she bemusedly beholds the world that sets her apart. As Joe Eula remembers: "You look into those eyes and suddenly you find yourself agreeing with everything she says."

But while everyone else had eyes for Audrey, her own gaze fell critically upon herself. Doris Brynner, who with her husband, Yul Brynner, met Audrey and went on to become her closest friend, says that "Audrey was a mass of complexes—she thought she was too flat-chested, she thought her feet were too big. We used to get together, and if she was in that kind of a mood, she'd say, 'Why can't I have small feet like you?' Which was ridiculous, because she was perfect-looking!" Like too many women, Hepburn considered herself "funny-looking," alluding to her crooked teeth, slightly broad nose, size ten feet, and elfin ears. "I never thought I'd land in pictures," she once said, "with a face like mine." Her fans, of course, clamorously disagree.

Audrey's companion Robert Wolders doesn't think Audrey had any awareness of how beautiful she was, because she didn't see herself as we see her. "She was, since her youth, so aware of what she regarded as her shortcomings, that she was flattered, extraordinarily flattered, whenever someone would offer a kind comment about her looks."

This divergence between how Audrey viewed herself and how the world saw her makes Audrey an "everywoman" of sorts—her insecurities, which we all share to some degree or other, make us feel more intimate with her. Nevertheless, when *we* think of Audrey Hepburn we don't think of any of the "flaws" she mentions above. If anything, we think of Audrey the way Truman Capote described his friend Babe Paley: "She had only one fault: She was perfect. Otherwise, she was perfect."

AUDREY ALWAYS LED a very healthy, disciplined life, and this, no doubt, contributed to both her energy and her attractiveness. She lived in the country, went to bed early, and took care of herself. "She always followed the program and her life was very continuous," says her son Sean. "She tried to get up and eat and take her walks and go to sleep at the same hour."

There were few secrets to Audrey's beauty. "My life isn't theories and formula," Audrey explained. "It's part instinct, part common sense. Logic is as good a word as any, and I've absorbed what logic I have from everything and everyone—from my mother, from my training as a ballet dancer, from *Vogue* magazine." The best word to describe Audrey's beauty regime is holistic—she listened to what her body needed, and saw that she got it. "In the city," she said, "one tries to live as though one were on a farm—that is, naturally: You try to exercise, but you can't always; you eat the things that are good for you, but you also eat things that are not good for you. Let's face it, a nice creamy chocolate cake does a lot for a lot of people; it does for me." You could say that Audrey's only rule was not to have any rigid rules. "You have to be as relaxed as possible about food and fitness and the rest of it, or you'll be a slave to your beauty habits. . . . You may have great skin, but you'll become a robot."

Ultimately, beauty is more than skin deep. As makeup artist Kevyn Aucoin, who worked with Audrey and has seen more than his share of cover girls, stars, and divas puts it, "The lesson from Audrey is that she faced her life with as much optimism and courage as she could." This contributed greatly to her beauty—both inside and out.

Also, unlike with most movie stars, Audrey's "look" was gloriously low maintenance. In a 1953 press release put out by her publicist, Audrey is asked what shade of powder she wore. "None." Lipstick? "Pale shades at all times." With her low-key lips and emphasis on her eyes, Audrey's makeup was clean and practical, a look that could be worn every day by women of any age.

For such an extraordinary-looking woman, Audrey claimed to have few beauty tips. "I'm not one who has rules," she admitted to *Vogue*. "I am not a

person who must have so many hours sleep so that my skin will look good. I love to walk, so I do get lots of air . . . lots and lots of oxygen. And I sleep marvelously well. I need eight or nine hours to make me completely happy; otherwise I long for a nap. But if I don't have one, it doesn't destroy me. I'm very relaxed and unmethodical about myself. I do what I have to do and let it go at that."

Alberto de Rossi, who did Audrey's makeup for *Roman Holiday* and worked with her throughout her career, had his own strong ideas about Audrey—and makeup. "Every time I see a face," he said, "I see what God has given it. But the look must be natural, nothing hard, never a mask. Never!" Like many actresses, Audrey grew close to her makeup man, becoming good friends with Alberto and his wife, Grazia. When someone once said that she had the most beautiful eyes in the world, Audrey replied, "Oh, no—the most beautiful eye *makeup* perhaps, but all the credit belongs to Alberto."

One of the techniques Rossi used on Audrey was, after cleansing her face with soap and water, to spread a light patina of foundation over her face and neck. He then applied powder, brushing away the surplus and spraying on Evian water, letting it set for two minutes before blotting with a tissue. This gave her skin a glowing texture.

Although Alberto worked with all the major stars, including Elizabeth Taylor, Ava Gardner, and Burt Lancaster, he always felt Audrey was special. "Audrey's bones are photogenic," said Alberto. "She has a very strong jawline. In a sense I reversed her face by emphasizing her temples. Except for that, she has such beautiful bone structure that her features need very little shading."

Away from work, Audrey didn't wear much makeup. "Only on my eyes—black liner and mascara, dark-brown eyebrow pencil. I use a brownish shadow in the crease of the eyelid and leave the brow itself natural." Sometimes, at night, she put a little opalescent highlight on the bony part below the eyebrow. She tried greens and purples, but they didn't suit her. As we first saw in *Roman Holiday*, Audrey always used a very pale pink lipstick, and the impression of no base or foundation. "I prefer an unmade-up look," she said, "simply because it's better for me."

The beauty of Audrey's look is that it still "works" today, and best of all, it is easily attainable. Kevyn Aucoin, who did her makeup for several shoots and public events, feels that "imitation is the sincerest form of flattery, and I think that a lot of people want to emulate her beauty and her style." Audrey's look, says Aucoin, is very simple. "A few tips would be to accentuate the eyeliner on top of the eye, keep the brow full, and use pale lipstick color. Those are the three big tips I would give as far as trying to recreate the *feeling*. I mean, no one will ever be Audrey Hepburn again no matter how many look-alikes there are, but that's one way to do it."

Having worked in the theater, Audrey had seen what not removing makeup can do to the skin, so she was fastidious about cleaning her face. A self-described "soap-and-water girl," she used Erno Laszlo products. But there was nothing exceptional that she put on her face at night, no special trick (unless, of course, one counts using a $25 bar of black soap). "I don't believe in fads," she said, "I do believe that good health is the key to good skin; if your skin isn't good, it's a signal that something is wrong."

Audrey had fine hair and favored shampoo from the London trichologist Philip Kingsley. She washed her hair herself every four or five days, put it up in rollers, and dried it under a stationary hair dryer she kept at home, since salons made her restless. She always used bath oil—l'Interdit or Floris. She didn't know if it did anything for the water or her skin, but she adored a pretty-smelling bath.

In terms of exercise, Audrey thought of herself as an outdoors person, without being the least bit athletic. She loved to walk in the country—to be out in the clear air. She walked for miles by the sea but never really sunbathed, since she got too hot lying in the sun. (Years later she said, "I don't turn dark but I do tan a little. It's probably just as well in view of what one hears about sun and skin.") She swam occasionally but didn't do anything by the clock. She didn't ski or play tennis or golf; with all those years of dancing and making movies, she said, she'd never had the time to learn properly. She did, however, have a massage three times a week, cautioning that it was important to find the right masseur, since a "bad massage can break down muscle and ruin you for life. A good one gives you a lot of muscle tone."

Audrey loved to cook and eat, possibly because meals were a way to bring her family together and show her love for them. "She cooked like she looked," says Audrey Wilder. "She was a healthy cook." Audrey herself said she preferred "healthy food, not health food—fresh fruits and vegetables and meats." She felt strongly about quality and quantity. She also thought too many

people ate too much. "I'm one of the healthy ones," she admitted, "I seem to have a sort of built-in leveler. I've a tremendously good appetite—I eat every-thing, everything—but as soon as I'm satisfied, a little hatch closes and I stop."

At home Audrey didn't like fancy food. She much preferred a simple meal that was exquisitely done—a perfectly cooked steak, a beautiful salad, some raspberries. When she entertained ("which is not, please, capital-E entertain"), she would have six or eight friends over for a dinner of, say, spaghetti, a mixed salad including whatever was in season, and a lovely choco-late mousse for dessert. Doris Brynner, who lived near Audrey in Switzerland, remembers that Audrey loved pasta. She also admits that as a treat when their husbands were away, the two women would indulge in vanilla ice cream with chocolate fudge sauce.

Of course, makeup, exercise, and diet are the least of what defines Audrey's beauty for us. What makes Audrey so compelling is not simply that wonderful face, but her innate grace and reticence. And her strength. Under-neath the gamine exterior beat a strong heart.

In Stanley Donen's *Charade*, Audrey plays Regina Lambert, a woman of a certain age and social set. In the opening scene she is having a quietly glamorous lunch on the deck of a ski lodge overlooking snow-topped moun-tains and contemplating divorcing her husband, when Cary Grant, as Peter Joshua, catches her eye.

"Do we know each other?" asks Peter.

"Why, do you think we're going to?" parries Regina.

"I don't know, how would I know?'

"Because I already know an awful lot of people, and until one of them dies, I couldn't possibly meet anyone else."

"Hmmm, well, if anyone goes on the critical list, let me know." Joshua nods his head and walks away. He's annoyed. And intrigued.

"Quitter," Regina says to his back.

He turns. "Huh?"

"You give up very easily, don't you?" she asks, laughing. The gleam in Audrey's eye is more than mere prettiness, even with Alberto de Rossi's assis-tance; it is fey imagination and a certain ability—in spite of Audrey's model's looks—to laugh at herself. Remember when she and George Peppard drop their dog and cat Halloween masks and kiss on the doorstep in *Breakfast at Tiffany's*? That takes a certain amount of je ne sais quoi. Or the scene in which Gregory Peck takes her sightseeing in *Roman Holiday* and pretends to lose his hand in the Roman ruin, neglecting—in real life, as well—to warn her of his trick? The jaw-dropping look on Audrey's face is priceless, and adorable. As Peck recalls, "Audrey was as funny as she was beautiful. She was a magical combination of high chic and high spirits."

Once you were exposed to her charm, beauty became, quite possibly, the lesser of Audrey's appeal. People loved her for her natural ebullience. From her first moment on stage in London in 1948, when she was just a chorus girl, third from the left in *High Button Shoes*, audiences responded in no small way to her vulnerability coupled with her good humor.

moon river

This look is all out glamour for evening. Take these tips from celebrity makeup artist DARAC for Prescriptives, and your lipstick will still be glowing.

lips

The lips are full and sensuous. First, line and fill the entire lip with lipliner to match lipstick color. Then, apply lipstick, blot with tissue, and reapply. Add a touch of gloss.

cheeks

Use a neutral contour color to help define your features. Apply color under the cheekbone, follow across the forehead, blending up into the hairline and down the side of the face and across the chin. Follow with burnt-apricot-colored blush, blending from the apple of the cheek back and down toward the ear.

eyes

The eyes are smoky and elegant. Brush a medium beige shadow on entire eyelid from lashes to brow. Follow with a smoky gray shadow across lower lid to crease. Line eyes with a black smudge liner, top and bottom. Follow with black liquid liner on top, applying more thickly at the outer edge for extra drama. Apply brownish-black shadow over liner and smudge upward toward the brow with a Q-Tip. By layering colors and blending, you need not worry as much about placement. Add a strip of false lashes for the Golightly glow.

sabrina

This look is youthful, empowered, and modern—a polished ingenue with a glint of worldliness. Try this look and you will be dashing around town in your own convertible in no time.

lips

Lips are very polished. Line lips with a lip-toned liner and fill in with a soft plum or mocha color. Follow with lip gloss for a glassy look.

cheeks

Cheeks are clean and modern. Sweep color across the cheekbone from the apple of the cheek to the ear.

For more pop, add a hint of pink blush on the apples of the cheeks.

eyes

Here, the eyes have it! Apply a medium plum shade on the crease of the lid. Follow with a soft, light violet beige across the entire lid, then softly brush it under the brow. For evening, add a dark plum shadow to the upper outer lid and softly blend inward. With a Q-Tip, smudge charcoal eyeliner across the entire top and bottom of the eye. Fill in the brows, giving them a strong arch and definition.

For a more dramatic look, line the inside lower eyelid with white pencil, and add a few individual false lashes on the outer upper lid.

fair lady

For public events, this is a look that Audrey went with her whole life. Follow DARAC's advice, and you will naturally put your best face forward.

lips

Lips are very creamy and moist in a soft rose or coral. The liner should be as close to your natural lip tone as possible. Be sure to line after applying lipstick for a softer look, giving balance and definition.

cheeks

DARAC prefers a sheer cream blush applied from the apple of the cheek down and back in a circular motion. For a healthy, outdoor look, apply a dot of blush wherever the sun would kiss you first—the bridge of the nose, chin, and over the brow bone.

eyes

Cover the entire lid with a soft warm beige shadow. Line the entire lid on top and bottom with a cocoa pencil and smudge as close to lashes as possible. With a Q-Tip, blend a small amount of coffee-colored or dark gray shadow over the liner and blend upward. This will give you a sheer, smoky look.

For evening, use a Q-Tip to apply a small amount of your darker shadow on the outer edge of the lower lid and blend up. Finally, apply a soft black mascara to top and bottom lashes. Finish this look with a soft rose or peach finishing powder.

country morning

Audrey loved her life in the country—casual, serene, and cozy, with time for good meals and good friends. This is a look for anyone, at any time of the year. When you dream of kicking off your shoes and walking barefoot in the grass—try a few of DARAC's tips and perhaps you too can pick up some of her effortless style and grace.

lips
Lips are very sheer. Apply color with fingertips and blend softly out to the edges.

cheeks
For this look, the blush is very transparent, blended only down from the apple of the cheek and back. DARAC uses a small wedge-shaped sponge for the most natural effect. Dip a large powder brush in a small amount of loose powder and then into the blush color before blending on the cheeks. This disperses color and creates a more natural application.

eyes
The eyes are very soft. Sweep a neutral beige or brown directly on the lid and blend down and outward. Apply a small amount of darker shadow with a small brush, as the liner, as close to the lashes as possible. Follow with a gentle coat of brown mascara. Brush brows into place with a small dusting of hairspray on a soft toothbrush. Brush up and out.

Audrey came to immediately wanted including me—and I

town and everyone
to lose ten pounds,
don't have to.

AUDREY WILDER

off to see the world

THE YEAR WAS 1961, and *Breakfast at Tiffany's* had thousands of women, a veritable army of Audreys, scurrying around in trim black evening dresses, "Moon River" wafting through their heads, searching for their George Peppard. The movie's influence was so pervasive that the ASPCA reported an avalanche of requests for orange tabbys (fourteen different cats were used for the picture). Felines aside, the Hepburn-Givenchy partnership reached the apogee of *rafiné* elegance as Holly Golightly's hangover chic caused a run on triple-strand faux pearl necklaces, sleeveless dresses, and oversized dark sunglasses that continues to this day.

The shooting of *Breakfast at Tiffany's* brings an abundance of stories from the people who were there. Letitia Baldrige, who went from being Jacqueline Kennedy's Chief of Staff at the White House to working as Tiffany's first public relations director, remembers that everyone adored Audrey. "She was equally gracious to the night watchman and the people who worked on the floor, as to [the chairman and CEO of Tiffany's] Walter Hoving."

Tiffany & Co. was almost as important a character in the movie as Audrey, George Peppard, and Buddy Ebsen. The production blocked Fifth Avenue traffic for two weeks, starting at five P.M. and continuing through the early morning, so as not to interfere with store hours. In the scene where Audrey and George try to have the Cracker Jack ring engraved, Walter

Hoving, conscious of the store's vaunted stature, refused to let actors work on the main floor. Instead, Paramount paid for all the real salespeople to join the screen actor's guild, save for John McGiver, the lone character actor who waits on Hepburn and Peppard. In any event, everyone was on good behavior around the millions of dollars' worth of baubles, since not one piece of jewelry was reported missing after the production returned to Hollywood.

In terms of the film's fashion, Baldrige remembers that Ohrbach's did a knockoff of Audrey's burnt-orange Givenchy coat with the half-tie belt in back that she wore on her date with Peppard. And as for her mink hat, "Everyone wanted one!" exclaims Baldrige, still rhapsodic at the memory.

Legendary fashion editor Carrie Donovan also met Audrey about this time. "Mrs. Vreeland [then the editor in chief of *Harper's Bazaar*] adored her," she remembers, "and my job was to carry out whatever Mrs. Vreeland came up with, so one day she said that Audrey Hepburn was going to be in town, and she was going to Switzerland, and she needed a wardrobe of clothes for skiing, for the skiing life, for St. Moritz.

"So I checked out the market, and assembled a collection, and she was staying at the Regency, so I arrived there with my selection . . . and she *couldn't* have been sweeter! So gracious! Beyond gracious! Heavenly! And I mean, she was at the *height* of her popularity, and I was just a helper!

"One of the pieces, I remember, was a pink wool pantsuit by Blass with mink trim, and these clothes were no more what she wanted to wear than the man in the moon! I was just some woman from *Vogue*, and she couldn't have been more delightful. The next day she sent me a bouquet of flowers in a wicker basket for whatever small help I was able to give her—it wasn't much. Audrey was just so attractive and so nice. She had *enormous* personal style."

THE FOLLOWING YEAR Audrey got to show more of her personal style in Givenchy's meticulously tailored daytime ensembles with three-quarter bracelet sleeves and contrasting piping in Stanley Donen's *Charade*. A Hitchcockian escapade of a missing fortune left by a murdered husband and his unsuspecting spouse has never looked glossier—in fact, designers Mark Badgley and James Mischka of Badgley Mischka cite this film as one of their favorites, stylewise. "We've loved her movies since we were kids—the beginning of *Charade* when she was in that hooded ski outfit in St. Moritz is just amazing!" Mark Badgley continues. "It's interesting that even though she wore European clothes, she wore them in an American style—meaning, she was open, she moved in the clothes, she wasn't stiff. "

With Audrey Hepburn as the wife who comes home one day to an empty apartment and Grant as the stranger who assists her (we *think*), the movie stars Hepburn, Grant, Givenchy's creations, and the city of Paris. Audrey's pairing with Cary Grant was memorable for their sophisticated verbal parrying ("How do you shave, in there?" Audrey wonders, touching the cleft in Grant's chin with her gloved fingertip), but her real-life introduction to Grant was—without her intending it—even more unforgettable. As Audrey recalled, "Cary and I had never met before we did *Charade*, so there we all were in Paris, about to have dinner at some terribly smart bistro. As it was early spring, Cary, who always dressed impeccably, was wearing an exquisite light tan suit. I know I was thrilled to meet him, and I must have been terribly excited, because not ten seconds after we started chatting I made some gesture with my hand and managed to knock an entire bottle of red wine all over poor Cary and his beautiful suit.

"He remained cool. I, on the other hand, was horrified. Here we'd only been just introduced! If I somehow could have managed to crawl under the table and escape without ever having to see him again, I happily would have. Instead, I attempted my best under the circumstances. I apologized and apologized . . . while Cary, still dripping wine, nonchalantly removed his jacket and pretended, very convincingly, that the stain would simply go away."

Grant responded to the small mishap gallantly—the next day he sent over a tin of caviar and a card telling Audrey not to worry about the suit. In the film, Donen added an inside joke when he had Audrey's character "accidentally" fling a scoop of ice cream on the lapel of Grant's suit as they walk along the Seine.

Audrey and Cary, both stylish yet down to earth, hit it off famously, and their affection for each other comes across onscreen. In one of the film's famous throwaway lines—an afterthought added by Audrey—she invited Grant into her apartment. "Why don't you come in?" she asks graciously. "I don't bite"—a small pause—"unless it's called for." In another scene Hepburn weeps copiously on Grant's shoulder. Glancing up at him, she suddenly ad-libbed, "Look, I'm getting your suit all wet." His instant response was "Don't worry, it's drip dry."

Audiences loved the smart interplay between Hepburn and Grant. Critics called the film "an absolute delight." It was Donen's most successful picture and when it opened at Radio City broke all existing box office records.

A YEAR LATER, as the film is released, Mel and Audrey find themselves back in Paris at Givenchy's atelier, watching the spring 1964 collection.

On press day the staff receives Audrey not as a celebrity, but as an old friend of the house. "Isn't she a *darling?*" a British voice drawls as Audrey enters, smiling and ethereal, on Mel's arm. The room is packed, everyone sitting knee to knee, tittering with anticipation. Audrey and Mel perch close to each other on Louis XIV–style chairs at one end of the big double salon crowned with crystal chandeliers. The room is warm—bright yellow fans spinning above do little to circulate the air—and Audrey immediately shucks off her cropped jacket, revealing sculpted bare arms in contrast to her light wool tweed sheath.

Although the 1960s are well under way, the old niceties are still in place. Ladies wear their best dresses—Givenchy, if they have them—with daytime jewelry. Not surprisingly, members of the fashion press are in black. Gentlemen wear suits and ties. Chic little ashtrays on slim white stands to match the legs of the chairs are placed near loyal customers who smoke. Everyone is smiling— the models, the *directrice* of the house, Audrey. Mel, focused as a hawk, awkwardly straddling his little gold chair, holds a pen in his right hand to mark Audrey's selections. She smiles gently as a model glides by. The focus is on the clothes, not the audience. The thought of inviting a rock star, say, one of the Beatles, to view haute couture, or of the models becoming more famous than their clothes, is laughable. The designer—in this case, Givenchy—is God. His vision, absolute. "Adding a flower or piling on details is not couture," Givenchy declared. "But make an utterly simple dress with a single line, this is the key to haute couture." Now he shows them how it is done.

The show begins with a series of linen dresses—suits with deliciously contrasting rouleau belts, jackets shaped in the front, loose in the back; a range of neutral colors: oatmeal, beige, and putty; perfect little seven-eighths and nine-tenths coats, the hems perfectly cropped to reveal the bottoms of the longer dresses worn beneath.

Audrey leans toward Mel, whispering, "*That* little coat I'd love to have!" He smiles. Then she shall have it.

More brilliance walks down the runway: coquettish black cocktail dresses, high in front, low at the back with crossed straps. There are the vivid colors, too, that Givenchy is known for—china blue, zinnia pink. And the workmanship! Your heart breaks. No detail is overlooked—curvy extended shoulders for set-in sleeves, jackets miraculously shaped from within, contrasting hem bands on jackets, coats, and dresses. The fashionable crowd is rhapsodic at the magic Givenchy presents for them today.

"A lovely little dress. On Gloria Guinness it would be divine," Audrey says quietly, not taking her eyes off the model. More than anyone else watching the show, she knows the steep price of creating perfection.

Professionally, the 1960s brought an extraordinary run for Audrey, starting with *Breakfast at Tiffany's* and *The Children's Hour* (both 1961), and continuing on to include *Charade* (1963), *Paris When It Sizzles* (1964), *My Fair Lady* (1964), *How to Steal a Million* (1966), *Two for the Road* (1967), and *Wait Until Dark* (1967). In terms of fashion and style, the decade was High Audrey—here, we see Audrey at her most flawless, her most polished. Gone is the chauffeur's daughter and the uncertain refugee wearing homemade clothes. In her place resides a woman unafraid to show her beauty, and all she has to contribute, to the world.

As she and Givenchy create the pure emblematic style we most associate her with, Audrey can no longer believably play a girl living over the garage. There is something revelatory to be learned from Audrey, and that is the power of transformation. In *Vogue* fashion spreads for photographer Bert Stern and in her films, we watch Audrey blossom almost in front of our eyes, becoming the woman she was meant to be.

At this apex of her professional career, Audrey, perhaps more than any other actress, believed that her clothes contributed greatly to her success. "Clothes, as they say, make the man," she admitted. "But they certainly have, with me, given me the confidence I often needed." In *My Fair Lady*, Audrey described the "absolutely divine dress" that Cecil Beaton designed for the transformed cockney flower girl to wear to the ball. "All I had to do was walk down those stairs. The dress is what made me do it." When she put on the glittering beaded dress, she *became* Lady Eliza, and so, too, with the designs of Givenchy, which Audrey said gave her the confidence to become the women she portrayed on the screen.

"What has helped me a great deal with the part are the clothes. It was often an enormous help to know that you looked the part; the rest wasn't so tough anymore. In a very obvious way, let's say you do a period picture, whether it was *War and Peace*, or *The Nun's Story*, where you wear a habit. Once you're in that habit of a nun, it's not that you become a nun. But you walk differently, you feel something. That is an enormous help. And also, in modern-day pictures wearing Givenchy's lovely simple clothes, wearing a jazzy little red coat and whatever little hat was then the fashion—I felt super."

AUDREY'S BELIEF IN the power of clothes went far beyond the costumes she wore in movies. This faith, if you will, extended to her personal life as well. Years later she confided to Givenchy (in a comment that still moves him), "When I talk about UNICEF in front of the television cameras, I am naturally emotional. Wearing your blouse makes me feel protected."

Audrey's enduring effect on fashion rested, in part, on her ability to evolve with changing eras while remaining true to her singular vision. "Audrey's style is so simple and timeless," observes Christy Turlington. "And while she was fashionable and contemporary, I don't think she played too much into trends." Audrey believed that everyone has her own style, and "when you have found it, you should stick to it." She never wore designers' clothes straight off the runway, but modified them to suit her. She took basic, elemental pieces and made the most of them, imprinting them with her personality, sometimes by means of a simple accessory.

Another reason Audrey looks so timely today is that she practiced restraint in her manner of dressing—restraint in what she bought and restraint in how she wore it. In Vera Wang's opinion, "Audrey's editing of what she would and wouldn't wear was very rigorous, very much the way a fashion editor looks at an outfit." This restraint can, in part, be attributed to her background. A French shopgirl will spend an entire week's wages for an Hermès scarf, or the "perfect" shoes that last for years. Audrey had much of this extravagant European frugality. She was born in a time when women owned fewer clothes, but they were of the highest quality. A reasonably fashionable woman might have two dresses, a couple of suits, a handful of blouses, and (after the late 1960s) a few

pairs of pants, but each item was meticulously chosen and perfectly tailored. Audrey's fashion sense was rooted in this long-standing European tradition, where women invested in a wardrobe rather than bought scattered pieces.

Audrey's restraint can be seen in the style of the clothes she chose to wear as well. There were no Nolan Miller *Dynasty* surprises in Audrey's closets, for she believed, as Diana Vreeland did, that "elegance is refusal." When we think of Hepburn, there are no sequins and spangles. Instead, there is the graceful curve of a bare arm, an evening dress cut on the bias, a perfectly tailored suit. Even her lack of jewelry, save for the occasional diamond-studded pearl earrings, says volumes about her personal style.

Because of what Givenchy describes as Audrey's "enormous personality," there was never a chance that the clothes would overwhelm her. As they say in the fashion world, Audrey wore the clothes, they didn't wear her. And regardless of the strong line of a particular outfit, she always added a little "something"— bubble sunglasses, an elegant scarf, or a whimsical hat—to perk it up and express her individuality, whether she was in a glamorous, seductive, or amusing mood. As seen in the self-tie bows of the party dress she wore to flirt with the battling Larrabee brothers in *Sabrina*, or—in perhaps a more extreme case—even the all-white suit she wore while driving her red sports car in *How to Steal a Million*, Audrey, like Mies van der Rohe, knew that "God is in the details."

Audrey's lack of pretension in the way she dressed translated into a simple elegance that transcended fashion. "She looks so pure," says Audrey Wilder. "She doesn't wear jewels or furs like the rest of us, and half the time her only makeup is around those huge eyes of hers." This clear-eyed, down-to-earth outlook of Audrey's remained with her always. As John Loring put it, "Anything that was flash to her was not real glamour or chic. There was no pretension." Forty years before Armani, Audrey Hepburn taught us there is nothing more modern than the absence of excess.

Nancy Reagan, who first met Audrey during her MGM days, knows that in fashion, subtlety is the toughest thing to pull off. "I remember in one interview, someone asking her how you can get the Audrey Hepburn look. And she said, 'Oh, well, it's very easy. You pull your hair back, get a sleeveless black dress and big black sunglasses and hat, and there you have it!' Well," Nancy laughs, "of course, it takes a little more than that!"

But it is Ralph Lauren who gives the most direct assessment of Hepburn's inborn fashion sense. "You could take Audrey into Sears, Roebuck or Givenchy or an army surplus store—it didn't matter, she'd put something on and you'd say, 'It's her!' Very few people can do that. Clothes look great or not depending on who's wearing them."

Our search for Audrey and her style, then, almost becomes a Zen koan: We become most like Audrey not by following her but by developing our own sense of self, our own style. Pamela Fiori, editor in chief of *Town & Country* magazine, knows that Audrey's strength came from being true to herself and not by following trends. "You see people imitating her, and they are Audrey Hepburn clones—it becomes laughable because they are trying too hard. Imitation is not what she would have wanted. She would have wanted women to develop their own style. She just happened to have a propensity of style."

BY THE 1960S Audrey was at the top of her game. With the critical and commercial success of a string of films, she took increasing risks, playing a nun, a lesbian, a blind woman, and even a prostitute. It is a testament to her acting ability that audiences accepted her in practically any role. By 1963 Audrey was one of the most successful actresses in the world. Jack Warner paid her a million dollars—then an extraordinary amount—to appear in *My Fair Lady*. It was therefore quite a shock when, in 1967 after *Wait Until Dark* (where Audrey, directed by Mel, played a blind woman terrorized by criminals who desperately want a heroin-filled doll), she abruptly stopped making films to pursue what she considered her most important role: that of wife and mother. Turning her back on Hollywood, Audrey returned to the haven she had created for herself in Tolochenaz, Switzerland, at her rambling 1730 farmhouse, aptly named "La Paisible"—the Place of Peace.

But while Audrey was flourishing professionally, there was trouble at home. Rumors of the Ferrers' imminent separation had been hovering around them for the past decade; now, it seemed, their relationship was truly played out. Although it is impossible to guess what goes on in any relationship, part of it may have been that Audrey had moved beyond Mel's opinionated manner, or grew tired of always trying to placate him. Surely some friction must have arisen from the fact that Audrey's career so far eclipsed his own.

While she and Ferrer collaborated on several projects through the years—*Ondine* on Broadway (1954), the films *War and Peace* (1956), which was to introduce them as the new Olivier and Leigh, and *Green Mansions* (1959)— Audrey's star was clearly ascending. Alone. Although the projects Mel developed with Audrey were artistically creative, they were less than successful at the box office, the ultimate arbiter of Hollywood. It must have been heartbreaking for a man of Mel's ambition, talent, and drive to be thought of as "Mr. Audrey Hepburn"—after all, he was an artist in his own right.

Part of the difficulty may have been personality. In the business, Audrey was known to be a delight to work with. Her husband, on the other hand, usually merited a candid rolling of the eyes. "Mel was a pain in the *ass*," confided more than one photographer who worked with Audrey. "He was always hanging around and meddling with the picture." In Ferrer's defense, actresses in those days were not known to have a lot of "juice" in Hollywood, even those

with Audrey's star power. In the movie business you needed someone in your corner. You needed an enforcer, and Mel was the enforcer.

Robert Wolders, for his part, feels Mel's contribution to Audrey's career was incalculable. "Mel guided Audrey as a husband, not as a Svengali, as some people would have you think. And I think the years of their marriage coincide with the most successful years of her career." Audrey, believes Wolders, had a need to trust. "She could not live without entrusting herself to someone, to put herself in someone else's hands. I think when she married Mel, she more or less put her career in his hands, because she trusted him. She definitely felt that he was her husband, that certainly he would propose or suggest what was best for her." For all his supposed faults, this much is beyond dispute: Audrey did some of her best work when married to Mel.

Unfortunately, neither their best intentions nor Audrey's success were enough to keep the relationship together. While Audrey attempted to make

the relationship work for the sake of their son Sean, born in 1960, their union ultimately dissipated. Having been married thirteen years, enduring four miscarriages and increasing tension between their careers, Ferrer and Hepburn announced their intention to divorce in 1967.

By the close of the 1960s Audrey was one of the most famous women in the world. But in spite of her glowing professional life, the failure of her marriage devastated her. For while Audrey's emotional clarity made her a compelling actress, it also made her a more vulnerable human being. According to Robert Wolders, Audrey had a huge capacity for both love and loyalty. "Once she sensed that she could trust somebody, she'd do anything for them," says Wolders. "And if she were disappointed in them, it would be the end of the world for her."

Audrey's next film mirrored the personal growth and changes she was experiencing in her private life. In Stanley Donen's *Two for the Road*, made while she was in the midst of separating from Mel, Audrey and Albert Finney play a long-standing married couple, and show all the ups and downs, tension and love, of a modern relationship. "It was extremely sophisticated," Audrey remembered, "both in its exploration of the various stages of the man's and woman's infatuation with one another and in the way the story played out backward and forward in time." Many fans and critics consider this Audrey's best, most "real" performance. The film opened April 27, 1967, at Radio City Music Hall; on September 1, 1967, their lawyers jointly announced that Hepburn, thirty-eight, and Ferrer, fifty, would divorce.

Audrey was taking chances in fashion now too. For the first time, she decided that Givenchy was not right for the character in *Two for the Road*, and with the help of Donen and fashion coordinator Lady Claire Rendlesham, she flew to London and shopped the boutiques along Kings Road. She chose mostly Mary Quant for the picture, with a dash of Hardy Amies, Michele Posier, Paco Rabanne, and other mod designers of the day.

Two for the Road was a clear departure from the careful Givenchy suits and white gloves Audrey wore in films like *Charade* and *How to Steal a Million*. Instead, the public saw a new Audrey in everything from jeans, sneakers and a red crew-neck sweater; a nude-colored bathing suit; a red and orange rugby-striped minidress with oversized clear acrylic sunglasses to a black

patent leather pantsuit cut so sharply it would do Mick Jagger proud. Audrey even had a nude scene with Albert Finney, although, according to moviegoing dictums of the day, Finney wore white boxer shorts and a T-shirt, while Audrey kept the sheet firmly pulled up at all times, revealing as much décolletage as a strapless evening gown.

While Audrey found the decision to end her marriage to Mel extremely painful, once she had made it she was able to approach life with renewed zest. As Stanley Donen remembers: "The Audrey I saw during the making of this film I didn't even know. She was so free, so happy. I never saw her like that! So young . . . I guess it was Albie." In a very real sense, her leading man gave Audrey her joy back, and she always held a special place in her heart for their friendship. "Audrey cared for Finney a great deal," says Robert Wolders. "He represented a whole new freedom and closeness for her. It was the beginning of a new period in her life."

In later years Audrey would recall that *Two for the Road* contained one of her favorite scenes in all her movies. "That business about changing outfits in the car. That's something I've done in real life. Also that incident about sneaking food into the hotel because the dining room's so expensive, only to find out later that the meals would have been included in the price of the stay. That's happened too."

As Albert Finney recalls, "Audrey and I met in a seductive ambience [in] a *very* sensual time in the Mediterranean. We got on immediately. After the first day's rehearsals, I could tell that the relationship would work out wonderfully. Either the chemistry is there or it isn't. . . .That happened with Audrey. Performing with Audrey was quite disturbing, actually. . . . With a woman as sexy as Audrey, you sometimes get to the edge where make-believe and reality are blurred—all that staring into each other's eyes. . . . I won't discuss it more because of the degree of intimacy involved. The time spent with Audrey is one of the closest I've ever had."

Albert Finney opened a door for Audrey, bringing in light and laughter, showing her another way to live. But in reality, Audrey opened the door herself. Audrey was no longer the young woman who sat beside her husband, smiling and protected, as he checked off clothing selections in a French atelier. The world was changing, and Audrey was ready to change with it.

a fan's notes

"I have to be honest," sighs Jeffrey Banks as only a spurned lover can, "it was disappointing." He is remembering his first meeting with Audrey, sharing confidences over a quiet lunch in Chelsea one rainy afternoon. You have to understand, he's loved Audrey since practically forever. When he was eleven he made his mother sit with him through *Funny Face*—twice—at a revival house in Georgetown. "I know it's unfair to put all of that on someone," he admits. "How can anyone live up to that?"

Loving Audrey the way he does, Banks is as opinionated and as possessive as any beau. There is his take on *Wait Until Dark*, the Ferrer-directed downer that features Alan Arkin terrorizing a blind Audrey in a pilled crew-neck sweater—could she possibly look any worse? "No, I have not seen the play, and no, I will not rent the video!" *Sabrina*: "Nor did I go to the movies to see *Sabrina*"—his voice drips venom—"the *remake*. Because as far as I'm concerned, there is only one *Sabrina*—and she was in it!"

Jeffrey's introduction to his idol came about through a series of coincidences. At a cocktail party in the Hamptons during the summer of 1982, Jeffrey met John Rizzuto, the president of Givenchy America. "Do you know Audrey?" he asked Jeffrey casually, not realizing this was his dream to end all dreams. "I'll introduce you the next time she's in town."

The die was cast. Audrey's next visit to New York was to attend the Fashion Institute of Technology's retrospective for Givenchy in September. Jeffrey bought the entire table next to hers. Like the perfect beau, he brought a bouquet of roses for Audrey—it was a bush, really, a *tree*—from society florist Renny and hid it under his table. Between the first and second courses, Jeffrey was brought over to meet Audrey. He presented her with the flowers and she smiled, but she seemed . . . distant. "I mean, she was polite and everything, but her eyes were kind of glazed over." It is clear that the memory still pains him. "And, you know, it was this moment that I'd waited my whole life for."

Even his dinner jacket seemed a little deflated when he came back and sat down at his table. His friends knew he was disappointed and took him out to hear Bobby Short at the Carlyle to cheer him up. But even Bobby didn't do it for him. The princess had let him down.

The next day, at 8:30 in the morning (*ungodly* for the fashion world, especially after a night spent closing Bemelman's), the phone rang in Jeffrey's apartment. It was John Rizzuto.

"Jeffrey, I could tell you were disappointed last night."

"It's just that she wasn't the way I thought she'd be, and I guess it's silly to think that way. . . ."

"No, you don't understand—Audrey's

mother fell in Switzerland three days ago. She hurt her leg and Audrey didn't want to leave! She knew that all these people had bought tickets, not only for Givenchy, but also to see her. And she didn't want to disappoint them. She took the overnight train from Switzerland to Paris, took the Concorde over, and then she did the reverse the very next day. She called her mother like, five times over the course of the evening. That's why she was chain-smoking—that's all she could think about. I promise you, the next time you meet her, she'll be totally different!"

The sun broke through the clouds. Now he understood. "And of course," smiles Jeffrey, "the next time I saw her she was *totally* Audrey." So Audrey and Jeffrey became friends, seeing each other whenever Audrey and Rob visited New York City, a few times a year, generally for award ceremonies.

One time they flew in from Chicago, and Jeffrey arranged for two Town Cars to pick them up: one for them, and one for Jeffrey, because he thought they might be tired out after their trip. After Jeffrey met them at Kennedy Airport, Audrey invited him for a drink at the Plaza-Athénée. Jeffrey demurred, not wanting to be a bother. He is, after all, a properly raised southerner, well versed in social niceties.

Audrey seemed disappointed. "Oh, well, if you have something better to do!"

Jeffrey tipped the second Town Car and sent it on it's way. At their suite at the Plaza-Athénée, Rob started to unpack while Audrey and Jeffrey had drinks and caught up. They sat on the sofa and started talking, about fashion—Givenchy, who had just had a retrospective in Paris, Karl Lagerfeld, whom she thought was so bright, Ralph Lauren, whom she loved. They talked about movies, Audrey told Jeffrey that Julia Roberts was one of her favorite young actresses.

Before Jeffrey knew it, an hour and fifteen minutes had passed, and he thought: Oh, my God, this poor woman! I haven't let her go to the bathroom or take her makeup off or anything! Finally, he said, "Listen, I have to go, I really have to go. I'll see you tomorrow night at the awards."

On his way out he saw that some-one—a designer we won't name—had sent her a bouquet, and they were very sweet but sort of inconsequential looking, and he thought: Audrey needs more flowers. The next day he called up Renny and said, "I need a huge arrangement—I need this kind of flower and that kind of flower." He wanted an entire garden. "And I'm going on and on about all the different species and kind of things I want in there," Jeffrey remembers, "and Renny's being very quiet. Finally, at the end he says, 'Uh, Jeffrey, you've told me what room and what you

want in there, the only thing you haven't told me is what you wanted to spend.'"

"And I said—'Renny, it's for Audrey, money is no object!' Which is the wrong thing to say to that man!" Jeffrey laughs "I'm working that third job, I'm *still* paying for those flowers."

That night at the CFDA Awards at Lincoln Center, there were tons of people coming over to Audrey, and Jeffrey didn't want to interrupt, knowing it is rude to interrupt someone when they're eating. Besides, he was sure he'd see Audrey at some point during the evening. After dinner was finished, everyone went into the New York State Theater for the awards presentation.

"And just as I open the door," Jeffrey continues, "I hear someone shout my name—and I turn around and it's Audrey, and she took my face and kissed me *four-teen* times on each cheek. And, I tell you—if you had shot me right then and there, I would have died a happy man. That was it, that was the crowning achievement! She thanked me, she named every flower and said it was the most beautiful bouquet she'd ever received. Then and there I decided that I would send Audrey flowers whenever she was in town."

Jeffrey continued another three or four times (becoming one of Renny's best customers) until finally, they were at dinner and Audrey leaned over and said: "Jeffrey, the flowers have got to stop, I love them but it's getting ridiculous!"

And Jeffrey replied, like a Billy Wilder script, but true: "Audrey, there can *never* be too many flowers for you. . . ."

She spoke many
English, Dutch, Fren
and probably others of

languages fluently—
ch, Italian, Spanish,
which I am not aware.

STANLEY DONEN

italian **days**

THE FIRST THING AUDREY DID after her separation from Mel was cut her hair. Alexandre of Paris, the Frédéric Fekkai of his day, did the deed at his salon at 3 avenue Montaigne. Audrey tried on a number of wigs to decide on a style—a good idea for anyone contemplating a radical change. After cutting and setting her hair four times, knowing half the world would be parroting her, Alexandre arrived at a style he dubbed the "Coupe Infante '66." A questionable name for a haircut, perhaps, but a great look for Audrey. Although the feminine short cut appeared simple, Alexandre revealed the extreme workmanship behind it, as each strand was blunt cut, then thinned diagonally with a razor from root to tip, and finally polished with a scissors cut on the bias—all of which was essential to giving Audrey's coif the look, according to *Vogue*, of a "brisk little mane."

But even a great haircut was not enough to lift the ennui she felt after her divorce. With Sean, now eight, at boarding school in Tolochenaz, Audrey soon grew restless, alone in the house in Switzerland. With the encouragement of Doris Brynner, who hosted small dinner parties for her, Audrey began socializing with the nascent jet set. It was time for some fun.

"I've worked nonstop from when I was twelve until I was thirty-eight," Audrey explained. No longer having to wake up for five A.M. makeup calls, Audrey began appearing in the glossy social pages with some regularity. There

was the affair M. and Mme. Antenor Patiño threw at their estate in Portugal. Patiño, the tin king of Bolivia, chose his friends, art, and wine with the most exquisite care. This party was no exception. Eighty-two guests assembled for dinner, among them HRH Princess Irene of the Netherlands, HRH Principe Carlos Hugo de Borbon Parma, Doris Brynner (who brought Audrey as her guest), Mme. Livanos Niarchos, Princess Ira Fürstenberg, Mrs. Claus von Bülow, as well as a scattering of the younger Rothschilds and Hermès. After dinner, in a pavilion constructed especially for the fete, a thousand friends came for dancing. The women, mostly younger, all beautiful, wore stunning jewelry; the men, black dinner jackets.

IN 1968 AUDREY also found herself returning to the scene of her first success, Rome. There she stayed with her Italian friend Countess Lorean Franchetti Gaetani-Lovatelli, wife of Count Lofreddo ("Lollo") Gaetani-Lovatelli. Upon Audrey's arrival, Lorean's maid began unpacking her suitcase, carefully hanging the short Mary Quant skirts and dresses Audrey had discovered during *Two for the Road* in the guest-room closet. After a few perplexing minutes, the maid interrupted Audrey and Lorean in the drawing room.

"*Signora*," she said quietly to her mistress, "she must have forgotten some valise." Why? wondered the countess. "Because she has only blouses. I hung up twenty blouses."

"Those are frocks!" exclaimed Lorean as Audrey giggled, sipping her Campari. The maid had never seen such short dresses.

Italy was good for Audrey; she felt freer there, more open. The people were so warm and giving—and so passionate. They were quick to anger and even quicker to forgive. After her friendship with Albert Finney and her divorce, Audrey felt it was time for a change. She wanted her life to open up. She just didn't know how.

In June 1968 Audrey was invited to cruise the Greek isles with her friends the French industrialist Peter-Louis Weiller and his wife, Princess Olympia Torlonia. On board, Audrey met Dr. Andrea Dotti, a prominent psychiatrist and professor at the University of Rome. A relentlessly charming thirty-year-old bachelor who was used to being seated next to socialites like Christina Ford at the best dinner tables in Rome, he turned his attention to

Audrey. Compared to Mel, who had made so many demands on Audrey's time, energy, and spirit, Dotti made Audrey laugh. Cruising the sparkling Aegean, a shipboard romance ensued. "We fell in love somewhere between Ephesus and Athens," remembers Andrea. "We were playmates on a cruise ship with other friends, and slowly, day by day, our relationship grew."

Well, not too slowly. Having met in June, by September, Audrey and Andrea were seriously discussing a life together. Marriage to this Italian nine years her junior was the last thing Audrey's mother wanted for her daughter, no matter how accomplished or wellborn he might be. But then, she had not wanted Audrey to marry Mel either. Her mother wasn't the only one with reservations—half of Audrey's friends were for the match, and half against it. Doris Brynner just wanted her friend to be happy, while Audrey Wilder insisted: "They didn't go together! You look at two people and you say 'yes' or 'no,' and this was 'no.'" One of Andrea's brothers even suggested to Audrey, "Don't marry him, just live with him." As a world-famous actress whose every move (from haircut to fashion) was chronicled, Audrey knew there was no way she would be able to "live with" anyone in peace. In the end, everyone else's opinions were pushed to the sidelines: Audrey and Andrea were in love and committed to having children. Of course they would marry.

"Do you know what it's like when a brick falls on your head?" Audrey said of their whirlwind romance. "That's how my feelings for Andrea first hit me. It just happened out of the blue." On Christmas Day, Dotti presented Audrey with a ruby engagement ring and soon after, a large diamond solitaire from Bulgari. In the first week of 1969, they posted their banns outside the village post office in Tolochenaz.

On January 18, 1969, six weeks after her divorce from Mel was finalized, Audrey and Andrea were married in a private ceremony in the town hall in nearby Morges. Blissfully happy, Audrey wore a pink jersey ensemble designed by Givenchy, with a neat matching kerchief to protect her from the light drizzle that had begun to fall. Doris Brynner and the actress Capucine, who had appeared in the popular Pink Panther series, acted as her witnesses. After the ceremony Audrey called Hubert in Paris. "I'm in love and happy again!" she gushed. "I never believed it would happen to me. I had almost given up." All brides are beautiful—this bride was radiant.

In Rome the new Signora Dotti (who was entitled to be called Countess, but refused and was plainly listed as "A. Dotti" in the Rome telephone directory) applied herself to becoming a doctor's wife with the same relentless focus she once brought to learning her lines for Billy Wilder. Scripts still flooded her mailbox, among them *Forty Carats*, after the Broadway hit starring Julie Harris, and *Nicholas and Alexandria*, for which she was offered the title role. But Audrey turned them all down, committed instead to the role of an ordinary housewife. Audrey was determined to do everything in her power to make this marriage succeed. Since her career had become a bone of contention with Mel, she now turned her back on Hollywood and channeled her energy, instead, on the home front.

As a private citizen in Italy, Audrey moved beyond white gloves and Givenchy's jazzy little suits, projecting others' dreams back to them in a darkened theater. Wearing jeans and a white silk shirt, a navy pea coat, a scarf around her neck, and sunglasses, she was able to walk around the city largely unnoticed. Audrey even felt relaxed enough about her personal style to wear white Dr. Scholl's sandals on vacation in Hawaii. She was almost gleeful at her everyday life. "I don't have a secretary," she admitted. "I don't have attack dogs, I don't do parties or official functions."

Instead, Audrey rose early to see that Andrea had his breakfast and often walked to work with him; she helped Andrea measure the lithium for his patients; she met him for institutional dinners at the hospital when he had to work late. In the midst of this routine, four months after their wedding, Audrey and Andrea discovered—to their great happiness—that Audrey was pregnant. Determined to keep this baby after her miscarriages in the past, she took the advice of her friend Sophia Loren, who had spent nine months in bed to bear her child and, in the fall, Audrey retreated to La Paisible for the remainder of her term.

Andrea visited from Rome on weekends, and for a while this arrangement worked, but he went out during the week, continuing the incessant socializing that made him such a popular man-about-town before his marriage. While Audrey remained quietly at La Paisible awaiting the birth of their child, the press had a field day as Andrea was seen out late every night gallivanting with an ever-varying array of beautiful young actresses and countesses. All of Rome, it seemed, knew of his predilection for nightclubs, discotheques, and parties.

While Audrey surely knew of Andrea's social activities during the week, all that mattered to her was keeping this baby. Barely moving from the couch to her bed for five months, she gave cesarean birth to Luca Dotti on February 8, 1970. Their marital difficulties temporarily smoothed over, Audrey and Andrea were overjoyed and shortly returned to their apartment in Rome.

Unfortunately, once their baby Luca was born, the Italian paparazzi had no interest in encouraging Audrey's attempts at normalcy in her family life. She was quick to say there was nothing negative about her experiences as a film star, since she did not want to seem ungrateful. Once, Audrey was asked if there were any downside to fame. She replied not in terms of herself, but Luca, explaining, "The only time it was a little hard for me, I think, was when my second son was born. I was at that time living in Rome and I could take him nowhere—not to a park, not down the street. I could not put him on a terrace without paparazzi. That was very difficult because it was bothering the child— to have photographers jumping out from behind trees, and he'd be howling because he was so startled!" Shortly thereafter a friend who had a garden in Rome told her to bring Luca there, with other children, as often as she wanted.

Living in Rome, Audrey's life changed in terms of fashion too. Although her friendship with Givenchy never wavered, his fashions were a bit expensive for her now that she wasn't working quite so much. Besides, as a socially prominent doctor's wife, she thought it more appropriate to patronize an Italian designer. Audrey talked it over with Lorean, did she know a good dressmaker in Rome?

"Doesn't Givenchy give you things?" asked the countess, amazed that Audrey did not take advantage of what one assumed was a typical celebrity perk. Audrey shook her head. With her customary good grace, she had always insisted on paying for everything. "After all," she said, smiling, "he pays when he goes to my movies, doesn't he?"

Valentino Garavani was thirty-six when Countess Lorean brought Audrey to his shop at 24 Via San Gregoriana. In spite of his five-year apprenticeship with Jean Dessès, and two-year stint at Guy Laroche in Paris, business was slow when Valentino struck out on his own with his father's backing in 1960. A few months later, all that changed when twenty-eight-year-old Valentino met the twenty-two-year-old architecture student Giancarlo Giametti while on vacation in Capri. With the potent combination of Valentino's considerable talent and Giametti's equally considerable attention to the bottom line, things took off. Ultimately, Valentino went on to dress Jacqueline Kennedy Onassis, Catherine Deneuve, Nancy Reagan, and Princess Caroline of Monaco.

It was not surprising that Valentino became a designer—the eye, the attention to detail, even the artistic temperament, were present in his youth. Growing up in Voghera, in Lombardy, the son of an electrical supply store owner, Valentino was the neatest boy in school, his hair always combed and his uniform pressed. Unlike most little boys, he never looked messy. He always loved clothes and was hypercritically aware of the effect he presented to others, throwing a tantrum at the age of six when his mother ruined his gold-buttoned navy blue suit by adding what he considered a "coarse" butterfly tie.

As a designer, Valentino's passions were absolute: He loved flowers, pasta, and creating beautiful clothes for women. "I shouldn't like to go through life without flowers," he exclaimed. "I have a passion for peonies; I always look for a very big, spectacular one that comes from San Francisco." He ticked off his favorites: "I also like roses, cyclamens, snowballs, pink camellias, and hibiscus." Like Audrey, he adored pasta—"Nothing for me is better than a plate of thin pasta, *pennette* with tomato and basil sauce," he admitted. "I could eat it morning, noon, and night, at teatime, lunch, and dinner; it is so satisfying."

They shared the same elegant outlook on clothing too. "The excessive must rest a moment," said Valentino, and Audrey clearly lived this truth. "The importance of fashion," he once said, "is to make one dream a little, to soften one's imperfections." And Audrey agreed.

Their bond was cemented when they discovered that they were equally crazy about dogs. Valentino had a much-beloved pug named Oliver (the mascot and namesake of his secondary clothing line) that traveled with him everywhere. Oliver even had his own seat on Alitalia airlines, where the stewardesses spoiled him silly.

Although they were not as psychically linked as Audrey and Hubert, Valentino became a close friend, accompanying Audrey to parties and enjoying dinner at her home. Audrey trusted this dashing Italian with the profile to grace a Roman coin.

Unfortunately for Audrey, all the beautiful clothing and flowers in the world could not soften the increasingly obvious imperfections in her second marriage. To put it bluntly, her husband of seven years was still behaving like a bachelor. Indeed, Dotti had always acted as if his wife were an afterthought to his nocturnal activities. He later admitted: "I was no angel—Italian husbands have never been famous for being faithful. But she was jealous of other women even from the beginning." Audrey, for her part, said she did not expect her husband to "sit in front of TV" when she wasn't there. Besides, she said, "it's much more dangerous for a man to be bored."

There was a brief glimmer of good behavior when Luca was born, but Andrea's chronic partying, which the Italian newspapers chronicled with glee, did nothing to bolster Audrey's self-esteem. She desperately tried to keep the marriage together for Sean's and Luca's sakes, but her high-minded behavior of looking the other way did nothing to ease the situation; if anything, it may have compounded her stress. It was one thing for a man to have an affair, she raged at Andrea one morning when she had had enough, but it was quite another to see it flaunted in front of her practically every day in the gossip pages! "Audrey was humiliated," recalls Robert Wolders quietly. "It was especially humiliating for her to have a second marriage fail."

In 1975, on the advice of her dear friend actor David Niven (who didn't care for either of her two husbands), Audrey returned to work in British director Richard Lester's *Robin and Marian*, a small attempt to show Andrea that even if he didn't take her seriously, the rest of the world did. In addition, both Sean, now fifteen, and Luca, five, were huge James Bond fans and threatened to disown their mother if she didn't take the part and introduce them to her leading man, Sean Connery.

The story of middle-aged love rekindled when Robin Hood and Maid Marian meet after a twenty-year separation, *Robin and Marian* appealed to Audrey because every other film role she had been offered in recent years was "too kinky, too violent, or too young." After eight years away from the bright lights, Audrey was concerned how she might look onscreen. For security, she brought her longtime hair and makeup stylists, Alberto and Gracia di Rossi, who had been with her since *Roman Holiday*, as well as Luca and his nanny. Sean would join them as soon as school let out.

In Audrey's absence, moviemaking had changed. With the paternalistic studio system dismantled, movies were no longer shot sequentially, at the leisurely pace of *Roman Holiday*. Lester was determined to shoot the entire movie in Pamplona in thirty-six days (as compared, for example, to *My Fair Lady*'s four and a half months of principal photography). He never took more than two takes. "On *Robin*," he said, "I set out to shoot eight or nine pages a day. There were about fifty pages [set] under a bloody tree, so why not?" Although Audrey was concerned how she might look during the rushes, the rough screening of each day's footage, her fears were a nonissue, since Lester never viewed them himself.

For economy's sake, all the traditional old-style Hollywood perks like personal secretaries, chauffeured limousines, and expense accounts were done away with. (One cannot help but think of Billy Wilder and his wife in Paris during the shooting of *Love in the Afternoon*—they left the Hotel Raphaël in protest, they said, because the bartender could not be trained to make a decent martini.) Even the traditional comp, the canvas chair with the star's name on it, was gone. Audrey made do with one of the chairs from her tiny dressing trailer. Clearly, this was a far cry from sharing catered tea every afternoon (with a real British butler brought in for a lark) on the set of *Wait Until Dark*.

But Audrey was a trouper. This time she didn't have any glorious Givenchy ensembles to fall back on; her wardrobe, such as it was, consisted of sackcloth habits copied by British designer Yvonne Blake from medieval originals. In spite of the arduous filming conditions, the movie, when it came out, was a success. If she ever doubted herself or her ability to act, Audrey saw she still had the right stuff. Critics applauded her return. "We are reminded of how long it has been since an actress has so beguiled us and captured our imagination," wrote Jay Cocks in *Time* magazine.

A GROWN WOMAN NOW with two sons, Audrey learned a great deal about herself during her Italian interlude and—through trial and error—about what she needed to ensure her happiness. She learned the vital lesson that the freedom to make your way in the world entails both the courage to dream and the greater courage to make mistakes. In the past ten years she had done both. By 1976 her marriage to Dotti was fraught with difficulties and disappointments, stemming largely from his infidelities. Four years later both parties showed "an avalanche of good manners" as Audrey formally separated from Andrea. Another chapter, with much hard-earned knowledge and a son they both loved to show for it, had ended.

As fate—or luck—would have it, Audrey met Robert Wolders, the man she would come to call her soulmate, during the winter of 1980. Of course, it didn't happen right away. After the excruciating highs and lows of her romantic drama with Dotti, Audrey was understandably gun shy. They met at her dear friend Connie Wald's home in Beverly Hills, a gray stone house that seems more Connecticut than California, with a white picket fence, masses of carefully tended rosebushes bordering the front lawn, and a discreet brass plate announcing "Wald" on the front door. It was a joyful, private place where Audrey felt comfortable, using it as her base whenever she came to California. "She took the stairs two at a time at Connie's," remembers a friend who visited her there.

The Wald home still stands today much the same as it did twenty years ago. With the accoutrements of Old Hollywood, there is a screening room that seconds as a living room during the day, one or two serious paintings in the dining room, the 1948 Irving Thalberg Award given to Connie's late husband, writer/producer Jerry Wald, a lap pool, and a guest house tucked away in the back, where Givenchy stayed when he visited Los Angeles. It is all very low key and comfortable, not at all glitzy—the kind of house where one has cocktails in the evening before dressing to go to a movie premiere or Ciro's. Built in 1936— eons ago in California—it is a house that seems to have been there forever.

In the quiet circles that run Hollywood, Jerry and Connie Wald, and later, Connie alone, were well known for their hospitality; a Saturday-night invitation for dinner and a movie was as coveted as any Oscar invite—probably more so, since it was strictly entre nous. Ron and Nancy Reagan, Billy and Audrey Wilder, Jimmy and Gloria Stewart, Greg and Véronique Peck, were all longtime friends and frequent guests.

Audrey and Rob met in Connie's wood-paneled den, with its fireplace, broad white couches, family pictures, and neatly labeled photo albums. "If these walls could talk," Connie says, smiling at the memory of decades of laughter. The den was practically as famous as many of the guests who gathered there for drinks before being called in for dinner. Rob admits that he considers that little den one of the most important rooms of his life. "Oh, they were fated to meet," says Connie, curiously choosing the exact same words used to describe Audrey's friendship with Givenchy. "Absolutely."

It was a sad time for each of them. Rob was mourning the recent death of his wife, Merle Oberon, while Audrey, realizing that her eleven-year marriage to Andrea Dotti was not what she had hoped, had begun divorce proceedings. Audrey listened, and shared her memories of Merle with Rob. Audrey and Merle had been friends for years, so Rob and Audrey had known *of* each other, had even said hello at passing events, but this was a quiet dinner party—no more than twelve, all old friends. It was the first time they ever sat down and talked.

They spoke Dutch, that gentle foreign language, discovering in the process that Rob had spent the war years ten miles from Audrey's little village of Arnhem. "America was like heaven to us," Rob said. "We couldn't believe such a place existed." Audrey agreed. And now here they were, Audrey and Rob, talking to each other in this beautiful home in Beverly Hills.

audrey's **closet**

"Some people dream of
having a big swimming
pool—with me, it's closets."

— A H

You might not be able to afford a Givenchy
original, but here are the basics of Audrey's
wardrobe to get you started. And what's
more, according to Polly Mellen, Audrey's
look is *doable*. "Her dress was not fancy
or bourgeoisie," she intones with the well-
bred vowels of a Farmington girl, with some
of her old boss, Diana Vreeland, thrown in
for emphasis. "You can't beat a black turtleneck and a pair of black pants. Audrey
Hepburn made that point—Audrey Hepburn
was black! She was very, *very* glamorous in
a sort of boyish way."

the essentials

The Little Black Dress—Where would
we be without the little black dress? Where
would the George Peppards of our life be,
for that matter?

A Sleeveless Sheath Dress—Classic,
classic, classic. Made for showing off tanned
legs. Not too much above the knees though.
In the winter, add sheer stockings and a
cashmere cardigan draped around your
shoulders.

The White Shirt—100% cotton or pure
silk, it can be long-sleeved, short-sleeved,
cropped, oversized, tied at the waist. No
epaulets, embroidery, gold buttons, or
fancy stuff—you're not in the military.
Unwrinkled is best.

A Jazzy Suit—We're talking a jacket and
skirt here. It needn't be a Paris original
(although that helps). Just make sure it's a
nubby material, sized to within an inch of
your life, and nipped at the waist. If your
mother's got a thirty-five-year-old version
from her glory days (you know the details:
lined in cool silk, covered buttons, a delicate hidden chain to weight the bottom of
the jacket), nab it.

Capri Pants—A bit of whimsy during the
summer months. In the fall and winter,
put them aside in favor of lean trousers fitted to your instep.

A Dark Turtleneck—Black or navy blue,
so you can make believe you're slumming
with Fred Astaire in the Latin Quarter—
even if you're just standing in line at the
post office.

One "What the Hell" Item—To show you
mean business. In her Hollywood years,
Audrey wore a mink pullover, with sunglasses, a scarf around her head, and lean
black trousers. Di-vine!

One Killer Dress—Remember the look on everyone's face when Audrey as Sabrina shows up at the Larrabees in that Givenchy creation? You can do the same—surprise your friends: Favor khakis during the day, an evening dress to break his heart at night.

Jeans, a Polo Shirt, Sneaks—For gardening and/or goofing around with the dogs, especially when no photographers are present.

Flats—Even a ballerina's got to take a day off now and then.

The Sabrina Heel—For that princess look. Worn barelegged or with sheer stockings and a sense of great expectation.

accessories

The (Preferably Hermès) Scarf—Invest in one and tie it every which way.

Dark Sunglasses—For hiding a multitude of sins.

As Little Jewelry as Possible (Unless You're Tagging Holly Golightly)—Make sure it's the best you can afford. With the right attitude, though, no one will doubt your cubic zirconia's the real thing.

A Small Dog with a Wry Name—Breeding helps and manners are optional, as long as your own are in good shape.

Gregory Peck

the basic ah-mo

- Wear your clothes, don't let them wear you.

- Ignore trends, you are above them.

- Study yourself and make the most of your assets. Everyone's got something wonderful to emphasize. Highlight it and ignore the rest. There's no point spending years in therapy "accepting" yourself. As the Brits say, "One must take the rough with the smooth."

- Get a good tailor—everything should *fit*.

- Think classic with a twist, never let your clothes enter a room before you do.

- Dress appropriately. The time to unveil your Sabrina ball gown is not when everyone's slumming around the backyard. Alternatively, unless you are Bob Dylan or Fran Lebowitz, it is disrespectful to show up at a major awards ceremony in a dinner jacket, jeans, and cowboy boots.

- Always look sharp. Audrey never traveled anywhere without requesting an iron from room service. And she used it too.

- Keep your shoulders back, listen intently, and *smile*.

- Count your blessings.

Audrey was a compl
adorable, loyal,
bright, dependable.
special sound
I tell you: Audrey and
graceful people

etely original creature—
elegant, sweet,
She had her own
and rhythm.
Rob were
to be around.

RODDY MCDOWALL

"The more there is, the less I
want. The more man flies to the moon,
the more I want to look at a tree."

la paisible

LA PAISIBLE WAS Audrey's respite, her solace—literally, her place of
peace. Bought in 1965 with her own money, the eighteenth-century farmhouse
in Tolochenaz, Switzerland, was, quite simply, home. With its extensive orchard,
cutting and vegetable gardens, and surrounding meadows edged in gray field-
stone, La Paisible was the place where Audrey could be herself. "There was
nothing even *remotely* Martha Stewart about that house!" exclaims television
producer Janis Blackschleger. "It was purely for her own personal enjoyment."

Audrey loved La Paisible and the life she lived there. Far from the
soundstages and rampant careerism of Hollywood, Audrey found her true
place in the world. As she grew older and gained some perspective on it, she
saw her life as a young actress as necessary; after all, it made La Paisible and
Hubert and all the glorious friendships possible, but it was also, she admitted,
"a rather circus life." Packing and unpacking, moving from one film set to
another, one *country* to another with little Sean in tow, traveling with fifty
suitcases, like itinerant royalty, which, in a way she and Mel were—the bed
linens, the silver, her white Limoges ashtrays, the contents of each trunk typed
and listed in a binder so she could find Mel's patent leather evening pumps
without any fuss. It almost made her roll her eyes, the life she lived then.

Switzerland was the antidote to all that—to the journalists with their
polite and inevitable impolite questions, the photographers, the fans, and, yes,

even the directors. Much as she loved Willie Wyler and Billy and Stanley and, later, Steven, that young one with the old man's eyes, she was thankful for a place where she could close a door on the world and its incessant demands. Tolochenaz was a good spot to get away from it all. Located above Lake Geneva, the town (with its population of less than five hundred) dated back to early Celtic lake dwellers. Now, along with one movie star, its current inhabitants were mostly farmers with vineyards and fruit orchards. But living there, Audrey was not cut off from modern society—the town's isolated, quiet charm belied the fact that it was a mere fifteen miles from Lausanne and thirty from Geneva.

At La Paisible, Audrey's loves were few and absolute. There was the house itself, the gardens, the dogs, her boys whenever they could visit, and the man she ultimately shared it all with, Robert Wolders.

Set back on Tolochenaz's only street, Route de Bière (down the road from the lone hardware shop and grocery store), La Paisible was a light, airy house constructed of peach-colored local stone, with French doors and windows, and beautiful rose gardens surrounding it. Inside, Audrey's decorating style, like her taste in clothing, was (as Audrey Wilder put it) "low-fat." In designing a room, Audrey favored white walls, floors, and couches, with clear accents of color— blue, green, even orange. There was something about Audrey and white—she adored it. In the mid 1960s her friend Deborah Kerr visited Audrey and Mel at their home on the Spanish Riviera near Marbella. "It was a charming house, very simple, and of course, everything was white. Wherever they went, everything was white. I always thought that was so indicative of her. Everything had to be white. The car was white. Even the baby was dressed in white."

Decorated in white wicker furniture, with masses of flowers from the garden, silver-framed photographs of friends and family (tellingly, her signed Cecil Beaton portrait from *My Fair Lady*, taped crookedly in its frame, is placed behind all the other pictures on the living room sideboard), and the occasional Daumier bronze, La Paisible is a nine-bedroom stone villa that could have gotten away with some heavy-duty antiques, some Colefax and Fowler chintz, for example, or a Chippendale highboy that quietly (or not so quietly) announced its provence.

Instead, Audrey's La Paisible had the greatest assets money can buy— space, sunlight, and peace of mind. Audrey decorated for herself, not for the image of a world-famous actress. The overwhelming mood of La Paisible is one of tranquility, perhaps hoping to recapture the peace that eluded Audrey in her childhood. "You go back," she said, "you search for what made you happy when you were smaller. We are all grown-up children, really. . . . So one should go back and search for what was loved and found to be real." At La Paisible, Audrey took her dream of home and made it manifest; her confidence and experience, her love of family and friends, speak from every room, without the ersatz (and ultimately withering) perfection of a professional decorator.

At La Paisible, life itself was important. Hours were spent shopping for, preparing, and enjoying meals. It was clear that one didn't interrupt lunch for something as inconsequential as, say, a phone call. Audrey took the time to set a lovely table; she loved her bright linen and china, with a small vase of flowers to anchor the setting. When the weather was good, and even sometimes when it wasn't, meals were taken outside on the back courtyard, the scent of lavender wafting up from the purple-tipped bushes lining the walkway, the dogs barreling around like maniacs on the grass.

Friends of Audrey's shake their heads at the mention of those Jack Russell terriers, a breed Audrey had first grown to love in Italy. ("Those dogs yapped their heads off!" confides one sotto voce, as if Audrey might somehow hear him.) At one time there were five—Missy, Tuppy, Penny, Piceri, and Jackie, then, after three of them died, just Missy and Tuppy. Unlike Famous and Ip, the deer, Missy and Tuppy got along well when Audrey was there and, needless to say, had the run of the entire house and all the couches. "My little hamburgers," Audrey called them. They slept on their mistress's bed—Porthault sheets be damned—because, Audrey joked, she couldn't find a basket big enough for all of them.

Audrey, like Givenchy, loved flowers, and her favorite day was spent out in the garden. Giovanni Orunescu, the brother of Audrey's housekeeper Giovanna (who had been with her for over twenty years), helped with the heavy yard work. In its generosity and abundance, the gardens of La Paisible reflected Audrey as much as the inside of the house did. She planted what seemed like acres of basil for the pesto she loved (along with tomatoes for pasta sauce) and gave bunches of it to friends to take home after they had been visiting.

When she first saw the house in 1965, standing on the roof of a friend's car at the base of the garden, she looked over the wall and saw the orchard in full bloom. She felt butterflies in her stomach, knowing she would live there. La Paisible's orchards had cherry, pear, apple, and peach trees, as well as berries, walnut trees, and even hazelnut bushes. Audrey loved all kinds of flowers—in the cutting garden were country daisies, hydrangeas, crocuses, dahlias, lily of the valley, and so many other flowers that only she and Giovanni could keep track of them all. On her sixtieth birthday Givenchy surprised her with sixty pink "Elizabeth" rosebushes, planted in an allée.

The garden reflected Audrey's whimsical, imaginative nature—she spent so much time there, she couldn't help but leave her imprint. She preferred a looser, more textured English-type garden to the formal geometry of the French. As always, Audrey had the inner confidence to do what she considered best, regardless of the current style. She grew corn in her vegetable garden, for example, then planted roses in front of the Indian crop. A friend who saw it remembers how striking, how prosaic, the mixing of the two looked. He had never considered it before, and yet, it worked. "How Audrey," he thought to himself.

WHILE LA PAISIBLE WAS HOME for her spirit, in 1980 Audrey found a home for her heart with Dutch-born actor and businessman Robert Wolders. Shortly after they met she told a friend she had finally met "her spiritual twin, the man she wanted to grow old with." It would not be stretching the truth to call them soulmates. They had the same sensitivity, the same dark eyes, and, before they knew you, the same careful way about them. After they trusted you, the same playfulness emerged. With his tall, comforting demeanor, Rob was the straight man to Audrey's cutups.

Robert Wolders is that rarest of things in today's society: a gentleman. Discreet, charming, with penetrating eyes, he is the kind of man who refills your drink when you excuse yourself from the table for a moment. He immediately puts you at ease—even if you have met him only ten minutes earlier. Some men fear women, fear their beauty and their power, and consequently belittle them (curiously, in America, this passes as wit in certain circles). Other men simply love women, cherish their beauty and singular courage. Rob is one of these men.

In casual Los Angeles he wears a light jacket and tie, the final button of his blazer cuff undone, showing the mark of a tailor. When he takes his jacket off, the monogram is subtle: RGW; he is not a rowdy trader on Wall Street after all. "I started to dress better since I knew Audrey," he admits with a smile, recalling how she used to buy him scarves and ties, sweaters for the country. "How could one not?"

In late 1980 Rob moved in with Audrey at La Paisible. Both her marriages had been, in a word, disasters. If not disasters for her husbands, then surely excruciating to someone as finely tuned as she. There was never any question of Rob and Audrey marrying. It would be, said Rob, like dragging someone back to the electric chair and making her sit down again. Much as he loved her, and she him, it would never happen. He couldn't put her through that again.

Not surprisingly, Audrey's mother loved Robbie. Having spent the late 1960s and '70s in San Francisco working in a VA hospital and raising money for veterans returning home from Vietnam, she was now in declining health and lived with Audrey at La Paisible. Though largely bedridden when Rob knew her, Ella van Heemstra was still a commanding presence and made it clear she was happy about the fact that Audrey and Robert had found each other, particularly since they were both Dutch. As Wolders recalls: "When Audrey and I first started to be together, Audrey's mother was living in the house, and we became great friends. There was some tension between Audrey and her mother, because her mother was very strict and severe and had difficulty showing all the affection she felt, and she felt a great deal for Audrey, but she couldn't express it. So she would use me as a conduit because she knew I would convey all that she felt to Audrey, plus she was very tickled by the fact that we could speak Dutch."

Audrey's relationship with her mother—so vital to the woman she became—begs for further discussion. Leonard Gershe, who wrote the script for *Funny Face*, first met Ella in Paris while they were shooting the dance scenes. "The two most unnecessary things on a set are the star's mother and the writer, not in that order, so the two of us would go off and have a Dubonnet in a café. That's how our friendship began, and it flowered from there." Gershe knew both women and, like Wolders, saw their relationship close-up.

"[Ella] had great humor and so did Audrey," recalls Gershe, "but unfortunately they didn't have it together—they didn't share laughs. I adored her mother, but Audrey didn't like her very much. . . . Ella played the role of stern mother. She was a different person when she talked about Audrey—judgmental—and she took her role of baroness quite seriously.

"On the other hand," he continues, "Ella could be very silly when she wanted to be, and so could Audrey. But Audrey never knew that woman. They didn't know they were really very alike. . . . Ella thought Audrey was a wonderful actress, but she couldn't tell her that. She was very proud of being the mother of Audrey Hepburn. That was even better than being a baroness.

"Audrey once told me that she never felt loved by her mother, but Ella did love her, believe me. Often people can't tell the object of their love they love them; they'll tell other people instead. I probably would have hated Ella as a mother," Gershe surmises. "But I loved her as a friend."

In spite of their differences, Audrey never forgot all that her mother had given her—harboring her during the war, moving to London, and helping her early career to the best of her considerable ability. She always made certain that her mother had a comfortable life. Except for the years in San Francisco, Ella lived intermittently with Audrey, sometimes for months at a time. For the last ten years of her life the baroness lived with Audrey at La Paisible under Audrey's full-time care, and died there on August 26, 1984.

SO SHE AND ROB created a life—their life—at La Paisible. With the boys grown, and Audrey's mother gone now, it was just the two of them and the dogs. Audrey rose about seven A.M., breakfasted lightly on coffee with lots of milk and whole wheat toast with homemade preserves. Unlike Babe Paley and Gloria Guinness, great beauties of another era who kept up appearances at all costs, Audrey never wore makeup at home. "I hope you don't mind," she told houseguests, "this is my time." They didn't. If anything, they thought her more beautiful without mascara, lipstick, powder, or any other artifice.

Although her Holly Golightly character in *Breakfast at Tiffany's* would have you think otherwise, Audrey never coveted or wore much jewelry either. It didn't make sense—she was always doing something in the kitchen or the garden. One exception was a ring with small diamonds that Rob had given

her one year for Christmas. "We didn't marry, so you could say it was our engagement ring," says Rob quietly. And when Sean bought her some sapphires from his pay for his first movie job in Hong Kong, she had them made into a small ring. She wore both of them, together, on the pinky of her left hand.

Audrey didn't wear a watch. In fact, she hated watches. And yet she was always perfectly on time. How was she able to do this? "I guess I was sort of the timekeeper," Rob says smiling. But even before she knew Rob, Audrey prized punctuality, considering it a mark of consideration. Friends say this was part of the Dutch heritage she shared with Rob. Audrey always allowed herself enough time to get ready for an event, never rushing and frantic.

Audrey had a great trick for forestalling any last-minute panics. Whenever she had an important event, she would try on the outfit well in advance, always taking the time to step into the dressing room adjoining her bedroom, and fix her hair and put on the proper makeup, stockings, and shoes. From her Paramount days, Audrey knew that you couldn't just throw something on and expect it to look good; the overall presentation was vital.

From all their years together, Rob can remember only one outfit that didn't work for Audrey. Sean was getting married to Italian designer Marina Spadafora in December 1985 at St. Peter's Church in Los Angeles (they later divorced in 1989). Givenchy had made Audrey a dress that was very fitted on top, with a scoop neck and a skirt that came out in a poof. "It looked like an upside-down tulip," remembers Rob. Givenchy liked to put a bit of whimsy in each of the dresses he created for Audrey, but this effort might have had too much. "It did nothing for Audrey's figure," says Rob. "It didn't look right on her." Very gently—for her son's wedding was a big day for Audrey, and she had worked closely with Givenchy on the dress's design—Rob broached the idea that perhaps this particular dress wasn't right for her. They were staying at Connie's house and she diplomatically agreed. Audrey promptly got on the phone with Hubert and had another dress (a stunning clingy, albeit tasteful red gown) run up and shipped pronto to L.A. Ever resourceful, Audrey recycled the top of the Dress That Didn't Work into another outfit.

But while Rob may have been Audrey's soulmate, he was still a man, and hated shopping. When they were together in Rome, Audrey knew enough to leave him at a sidewalk café with his newspaper and cappuccino to wait for

her when she picked up some shoes from Ferragamo. "Oh, I can't stand shopping, I go nuts in stores!" he exclaims. Still, he used to attend Givenchy's private shows in Paris with Audrey from time to time. Those he liked.

At La Paisible, Audrey wore jeans and a Lacoste shirt much of the time, but no belt. She didn't care for belts, except on dresses; with jeans—never. She wore ballet-type slippers and occasionally sandals, or clogs for the garden. But even tucked away in Switzerland—playing with the dogs, or relaxing by reading Jeffrey Archer and Ken Follett, Audrey must have had some sense of her influence on women's fashion, and on women themselves. Well into the 1980s, when Rob and Audrey traveled with other couples (occasionally on a friend's private jet, when they were lucky), the women would arrive at the airport the way they did in the '40s and '50s, wearing good wool suits, matching pocketbooks, and even hats, because they knew Audrey would be there. Audrey, by contrast, would have on jeans and a T-shirt, with a well-cut blazer. Not surprisingly, she inevitably outclassed them, even if they did have their own planes.

WHILE HER FANS might eternally see her as the princess, Sabrina, or Holly Golightly, by the time Rob knew her, the exquisite clothes she had worn had been generously passed on to relatives and friends. If she needed a new gown for an event, she borrowed it from Hubert. Before her death, twenty-five of her dresses and evening clothes, enough to fill four trunks, were returned to Givenchy in Paris for his private collection. There would be no Sotheby's auction of Hepburn's personal effects after she was gone.

Audrey had lived her Hollywood life so fully and was occupied by the present so completely that she had neither the time nor the psychic inclination to moon over—or wallow in—the past. "I cannot look back with nostalgia at a coat I enjoyed wearing years ago," she admitted. "I was inside it and it kept me warm, but I am still here and the coat is something of the past. Or a photograph of me: I don't look at a photograph of myself fifteen years ago with regret or nostalgia, although I can be amused or fascinated." In fact, in 1992 Audrey mused that "I wish that early in my career someone had warned me, 'Now, one day people will be asking you for anecdotes about the films you made.' Then I might have started keeping a little diary and filling it with personal observations about some of the extraordinary people with whom I've worked and the times we shared." Audrey never kept a diary.

She was equally unsentimental about her film career. At a film retrospective in Holland in 1988 that opened with *Funny Face*, she said to Leendert de Jong, the organizer, "I hope you got a good print and that the colors are still bright." When was the last time she saw it? he wondered. The premiere. And Rob had never seen it. She and Rob happened to be home one night when *Breakfast at Tiffany's* was on television. Audrey especially liked the scene with the Halloween masks.

While she loved the people she worked with, and gave acting her all, movies played an insignificant part in Audrey's emotional life. "I cannot look back on a movie with the nostalgia I would have for a house where I have lived and been happy or sad, or a place I have been with my child. . . . Those are things that affect me emotionally." Indeed, the things Audrey loved best were Rob, her pets, her home, her garden, and, most of all, her two sons, Sean and Luca, whom she considered her "greatest achievement." Audrey once commented that "even when I was a little girl, what I wanted most was to have a child. That was always the real me. The movies were fairy tales."

IN JANUARY 1989 Audrey received a phone call from a producer in Los Angeles, Janis Blackschleger, who wanted her to host a program called *Gardens of the World*. Of course, she didn't know much about gardening herself, she told Janis quickly, she just liked to put on jeans and muck about for a few hours. Her favorite therapy, she admitted, was pulling weeds. Compared to an expert like Penelope Hobhouse, who would also be appearing on the program, what could she possibly contribute? Still, it sounded *divine* — to visit the world's most beautiful gardens with Robbie and share that experience.

Meanwhile, Audrey had begun doing small events for UNICEF, the children's rights organization of the United Nations. In 1990 conductor/composer Michael Tilson Thomas, head of the New World Symphony Orchestra in Miami, came up with the idea of having her read selections of *The Diary of Anne Frank* while he conducted an original orchestral work in the background. He had little idea how meaningful his suggestion was to Audrey.

Anne Frank had shadowed Audrey's life for many years. Audrey had

read Anne's diary prior to its original Dutch publication in 1947. It devastated her. As she told Larry King: "When the liberation finally came, too late for Anne Frank, I took up my ballet lessons and went to live in Amsterdam with my mother in a house we shared with a lady writer, who one day handed me a book in galley form and said, 'I thought you'd like to read this.' It was in Dutch, 1947: *The Diary of Anne Frank.* I was quite destroyed by it. . . . I was asked to do the picture and the play, I was never able to. There were floods of tears. I became hysterical. I just couldn't deal with it."

When George Stevens asked her to play Anne in the movie version in 1956, she begged off, saying that at twenty-nine, she could not possibly play a fourteen-year-old. In truth, she felt it would have been too wrenching to bring back the ghosts of those horrific times—the reality had been heartbreaking enough. Anne's story was, in many ways, Audrey's own. "I knew so many girls like Anne," she remembered. "This child who was locked up in four walls had written a full report of everything I'd experienced and felt."

In March 1990, in spite of her trepidation and with Thomas's encouragement, Audrey narrated the work, now entitled *From the Diary of Anne Frank.* Her first stage appearance in thirty-five years would be a series of benefit concerts for UNICEF, taking place in five American cities, as well as a performance with the London Symphony Orchestra in 1991. She hoped their efforts would pay tribute to Anne Frank's memory. And just as important, she knew it would benefit children.

Michael grew close to Audrey during their work together. Asked to describe her, he says, "She was the dearest soul I ever met or worked with. She had that quality of 'recognizing' you even when meeting you for the first time. She looked at you in those first seconds with a delicious surprise—as if, 'My dearest friend, you've suddenly appeared, how wonderful to see you again!' She made you feel there was some special secret you shared with her, some beautiful melody playing that perhaps the two of you could hear."

And, since this is Audrey, he has his own anecdote about her and her style. Just before the London premiere, Audrey was undecided about what to wear. As Thomas tells it: "She said, 'I can't decide if I should wear the pantsuit or the dress. Let me model them for you.' She went into the next room and came back wearing this very elegant pantsuit and struck some tomboyish poses. Then she got serious and said, 'Now I'll show you the dress.' She disappeared and came back wearing this stunningly understated Givenchy creation that hugged her gorgeous frame. I was absolutely dumbstruck. I just stood there with my mouth open, speechless. After a moment she looked at me very kindly and said, 'I guess you prefer the dress.'"

Through her work with UNICEF, Audrey aimed to use her voice, her face, and whatever lingering interest people had in her not only to help children, but also to give something back to an organization that had aided her in her direst need. Indeed, Audrey had been a recipient of the United Nations' largesse when relief came to Holland after the war. And now here she was, working for them.

Audrey well remembered the excitement when the United Nations Relief and Rehabilitation Administration (the forerunner of UNICEF) workers delivered food, blankets and medicine to the local schools, filling every empty building they could find. She went to a huge classroom, where she could pick out coats, sweaters, and skirts. "They were so pretty and had come from America," she recalled. "We thought, how could people be so rich to give away things that looked so new?" She remembered, too, the smell of English cigarettes when the soldiers liberated Arnhem. How she loved the confident laugh of the American GIs. She would always associate freedom with the smell of tobacco. Funny how life worked out—like meeting Rob, for example. If they had met when she was eighteen, she never would have appreciated him.

Interviewers always asked when they planned to marry, and Audrey responded with Willie Wyler's saying: "If it ain't broke, don't fix it!" And then she smiled, with the cameras rolling once more. She had so much to look forward to. Steven Spielberg called the previous week—he was sending her a script, *Always*, he wanted her to play a sort of angel, a good spirit. They would be shooting in Montana, a place she'd never been before. She didn't know if she'd take the role or not, she hasn't worked much since her retirement, hasn't needed to, really. She was as nervous and uncertain about accepting the role as the skinny ballet dancer in London who tested for *Roman Holiday* all those years before.

So who knew what the future might bring? It was impossible to plan. But with her boys raised and healthy, and Rob and the dogs, and Giovanni helping with the garden, these days at La Paisible were the happiest of her life.

in the kitchen with audrey

Few things exasperate Audrey's friends more than the anorexia rumors that swirled around her in the media. "Audrey *loved* to eat!," scoffs Connie Wald with a dismissive wave of her hand. "And she was a wonderful cook—she loved nothing better than to be in the kitchen with the children." Audrey Wilder agrees. "She was way pre-anorexic, that was just the shape of her body. She was a healthy cook, and she ate, there was no question about it!" Julie Leifermann, who traveled with Audrey for three months shooting the PBS show *Gardens of the World*, thought that Audrey had a wonderful understanding of proteins and carbohydrates, and eating to give herself energy. "She ate a lot of fruit," Leifermann remembers. "But she ate fairly simply, because she didn't want to bog herself down with huge meals, because we would be getting up early in the morning to shoot. When she was working or constantly traveling, her instinct was to eat healthy, and eat the things that gave her energy, with occasional indulgences here and there, but it wasn't anything you'd really notice."

What did Audrey like to cook? Pasta, for starters, which she no doubt refined during her years in Rome. In Connie's leather-bound scrapbook entitled "La Paisible," there are colorful photos of luncheons on the terrace, Sean's seventh birthday party, bright salads held by Giovanna Orunescu, the cook, platters of hot dogs (one of Audrey's all-time favorites), glistening string beans sautéed in olive oil, quiche on a bed of home-grown lettuce, raspberries with fresh cream for dessert.

Audrey liked Granny Smith apples as a snack, but mostly (and more longingly) she loved chocolate. She baked brownies for the cast and crew of *The Children's Hour* "with powdered sugar sprinkled on top," Shirley MacLaine remembers dreamily. Audrey also loved Swiss cooking chocolate, having one or two squares in the afternoon as a treat. "You know what it was with Audrey?" remembers Jeffrey Banks when asked how Audrey kept her figure. "She would eat anything and everything, but she wouldn't eat huge quantities of it."

In addition to the war having permanently altered her metabolism, Audrey was always very physically active. She was not the kind of person who sat around watching television when there was work to be done in the garden. She was fanatical about getting fresh air. After dinner she liked nothing better than to take the dogs for a walk. And these were not country rambles—Audrey *moved*. Houseguests not used to her routine were left practically panting in her wake as Audrey raced in the Swiss countryside.

According to her friends, Audrey didn't eat much junk food. There are no recorded instances of her ever stopping at

AUDREY STYLE

McDonald's, for example, although she, Rob, and Connie used to go to the Hamburger Hamlet on Sunset after catching a movie in Westwood. After their meal they always split the Ultimate Hot Fudge Cake for dessert.

So if you're feeling in need of a Hepburn-esque culinary moment, spread some homemade raspberry preserves on whole wheat toast in the morning (and slip some to your dog while you're at it), munch a Granny Smith apple, have some Swiss baking chocolate in the afternoon. For dinner, toss up some pasta with marinara sauce or penne alla vodka, and think of Audrey.

I don't think that
knew that when
appear in public
she was very
But she always pulled

many people
Audrey had to
and give a speech,
nervous, terribly nervous!
it off beautifully.

NANCY REAGAN

fair lady

APRIL 1990 FOUND AUDREY at the gardens of the Keukenhof in Holland surrounded by flawlessly planted beds of tulips, studying her lines for *Gardens of the World*, the PBS series she was hosting. Wearing trim white wool trousers and a soft lilac cashmere cable-knit sweater with a white shirt underneath, she added her own distinctive words to the script. "I think if God were to make a patchwork quilt, it would look like this," she said of the acres of tulip fields.

Audrey wore off-the-rack Ralph Lauren for the program. Givenchy was perfect for the White House dinners Nancy Reagan invited her and Rob to, but Ralph's daywear, so American, so stylish, managed in his incomparable way to convey much of what Audrey felt was important. As a designer, Lauren spoke to Audrey. "You conjure up all the things I most care about," she told him. "The country, misty mornings, summer afternoons, great open spaces, horses, cornfields, vegetable gardens, fireplaces, and Jack Russell terriers. As a man, I respect you for your total lack of pretension." Audrey could almost have been describing herself.

Lauren's regard was high for Audrey too. She had been his ideal ever since he saw *Roman Holiday* at the Loew's theater in downtown Brooklyn. When asked to work with her on the *Gardens* project, Lauren said, "Who wouldn't want to drop everything and design for Audrey Hepburn?"

To prepare for the three-month shoot, Audrey, Robert, executive producer Janis Blackschleger, and producer Stuart Crowner had a meeting in

New York City with Ralph Lauren and his creative staff. Audrey put on a private fashion show to make a final decision on the clothes she would wear. Audrey's artistic sensibility was so refined that not only was she wondering if the clothes looked good on her, she was additionally concerned that the overall look of the outfit match the particular garden she was visiting. She chose the palest pink tailored jacket and skirt with gently shaped shoulders for the famed La Roséraie de Bagatelle on the outskirts of Paris, while her visit to George Washington's gardens at Mount Vernon called for a trim, cream-colored jacket with gold buttons and a Nehru-style collar that echoed the ribbed bands of a military uniform.

Stu Crowner, who had never been exposed to the world of high fashion—or much fashion at all, before this—was fascinated with the interplay between Audrey and Ralph as they discussed her wardrobe. "They were like these two masters. It was clear to me that there was a tremendous respect between them, that they appreciated the talent of the other. And between the two of them, *nothing* escaped their attention."

A slight fashion faux pas that occurred that day also shows the innate thoughtfulness of both Audrey and Lauren. Knowing he had an important meeting with these fashion-conscious people, Stu bought a new outfit. As he tells it: "I thought I looked great! Our meetings went really well, and after it was all over, I went back to the hotel room, took off my jacket, threw it on the bed." Crowner laughs, remembering what happened next. "And there was this enormous *price tag* sewn into the underarm of the jacket. They must have known! Because I must have raised my arm to make a point, but they were too gracious to say 'excuse me,' because they knew it would have embarrassed me."

Audrey and Ralph's friendship extended beyond the *Gardens* project, as she and Rob later visited the Lauren family in Jamaica. The two couples even shared a pizza in their hotel suite at the posh Plaza-Athénée one night after Audrey called Ralph on the spur of the moment and invited him and his wife, Ricky, to watch the Academy Awards. Audrey and Ralph sat on the floor like college freshmen with Rob and Ricky, munching pizza, sipping room-service beer, and cheering their favorites.

Audrey was Blackschleger's first choice to host the garden series. "*Gardens* and Audrey was such an obvious match," she says. "We said the name 'Audrey

Hepburn' and people's faces just lit up!" And although the budget was a concern, Crowner says that, "we fully expected to support a star of her magnitude with the support system of hair and makeup, and because it was her, we were going to have the same people travel with us. That was $200,000 to 300,000 added to the budget. We called Audrey and asked if there was anyone she liked to travel with to help her with her wardrobe, and hair and makeup, and she gave us a few names, someone she worked with on *Always*, the Steven Spielberg movie. So we started negotiations, and raising the money from PBS, and it was really expensive."

About three weeks later, the producers got a call from Audrey who said, "You know, I was thinking, if you could get me a hairdryer every fourth day wherever we are, and an ironing board and an iron, I'll do my own hair and I'll do my own makeup and I'll do my own wardrobe." Blackschleger vetoed the idea.

"I like to iron," persisted Audrey. "You *can't* iron," said Blackschleger, imagining how it would look if word got out that a producer was asking the beloved Miss Hepburn not only do her own hair and makeup, but her own ironing! This was a woman who had been nominated for five Oscars—this wasn't an NYU film school project. "No, no," Audrey laughed over the phone from Switzerland, "I like to iron!"

So Audrey ironed. Stu Crowner has an image of knocking at her door at 5:00 in the morning to pick her up, Robbie opening the door and there she was—ironing her Ralph Lauren skirt. He thought, perhaps, she looked at it as a mark of independence from having hairdressers and makeup people fussing over her.

Since they spent so much time together in fairly close quarters during the *Gardens of the World* shoot, the producers and crew were able to see what Audrey was "really" like. Her professionalism made her a joy to work with. As Janis remembers, "She was always on time and ready to work. She knew her lines, in fact, her suggestions elevated the lines—she could give lessons on celebrity behavior." Coordinating producer Julie Leifermann, whose main job was to assist Audrey on the road, also grew close to her. She agrees with Janis: "Having known Audrey, I have less tolerance for the star thing, and she was responsible for me having less tolerance—if Audrey Hepburn can live on the road for three months, and be more talented than 99.9 percent of anybody on this planet, and come in and be on time and know her material and be delightful and professional and give you gold on camera—when I come across that behavior now, I have a really hard time with it. Celebrities today need to go to the Audrey Hepburn School of How to Be a Star. She should have given lessons or written a book about it!"

Behind the scenes, Janis also saw that Audrey had "certain hats that she wore, you know, the signing autographs at the hotels. Everywhere we went, there would be hordes of people, at the Plaza-Athénée in Paris there would be people holding up old 8 by 10 glossies of her, and movie posters, they knew she was there. So, when the car would pull up, she would have to do the public thing. And then, get into her hotel and it was cocktail time!" Julie laughs. "First thing after she got out of the hotel was get out of the clothes and get into something comfortable—get into the jeans."

One reason Audrey looks so good in the series was her careful marshaling of her time. She and the producers worked out an arrangement where she would shoot four hours a day —two in the morning and two in the afternoon—because she needed to rest so she could look good. "And that worked for us," says Crowner, "because when you shoot outdoors, you don't want to shoot in the middle of the day because the light is too flat anyway. The best light is in the late afternoon, and the next best is in the morning. Audrey knew that. So we'd do other things in the middle of the day and then we'd call her."

Of course, not every moment went smoothly. Shooting at Hidcote Manor, in England, Audrey flubbed her lines a few times and the director was uptight. "I'm going to lose her, the light's going. . . ." It had been a long day, and he was a little testy with her. "*Okay*, Audrey, let's do it again." And this is someone who'd been directed by Billy Wilder and Stanley Donen! The British crew was wonderful, they loved Audrey. They couldn't have cared less about flowers, they just wanted the chance to work with her. In the midst of this tense moment, one of them gave some well-placed advice to the director: "Guv'nor—blame the grip, don't blame the money."

Crowner thinks Audrey's innate sense of grace that found its way into her professionalism came from her upbringing. "I remember reading," he says, "something about people who were raised in Britain's upper class, where they have been taught to be gracious, rather than in 1970s and '80s America—whatever's on your mind, go with it, totally unload everything! Audrey was very generous with her spirit and very generous with how you felt. In other words, she considered how *you* felt more than how she felt. I'm sure she took care of herself, her psyche, and her soul and all those things, but it wasn't at the expense of her friends or colleagues."

"I have tried to raise my kids," he continues, "with the idea of considering the other person as much as you do yourself. For example, if I answer the phone, I say 'hello' or 'Stu Crowner.' Audrey said, '*Hel*-lo!' '*Hel*-lo!' Now, the reaction that that would give the caller is 'oh, she wants to hear from me!' Which, of course, is nuts, because she doesn't know who is on the line. She

made you feel good, and she was doing that on purpose. Why does everyone say that she had this regal stature?" Crowner reflects. "I think it has to do with that generosity of spirit. If she didn't care about me, I didn't know it." He laughs. "You know? Maybe it was just a performance, but I don't want to analyze it because I just know it made me feel good after I spoke with her."

At the end of the shoot, knowing money was tight for the producers, Audrey and Rob hosted a dinner for the crew. To thank Lauren for his work, she sent him a carved wooden box with a picture of a rose from her own garden, that she had taken herself. When you received a gift from Audrey, you knew it was from the heart.

T H E   Y E A R   B E F O R E her *Gardens of the World* adventure, Audrey made a brief appearance as an angel named Hap in Steven Spielberg's *Always*. Dressed in casual slacks and a turtleneck sweater, a costume she and designer Ellen Miroinick worked out together, Audrey floats across a golden field, a vision in white with a beatific smile. Although no one could have imagined it at the time, it was Audrey Hepburn's final film role, and the one that most clearly mirrors her own spiritual philosophy. Adapted from the film classic *A Guy Named Joe*, Pete Sandich, played by Richard Dreyfuss, is a legendary pilot with a passion for daredevil flying who loses his life while saving his best friend. Now he must help the woman he loved find another love.

Steven Spielberg, who found Audrey "much more down to earth than I expected," during the ten-day shoot, remembers that the writers worked closely with her to get her voice. "It's what flyers and piano players and everyone else count on," Hap counsels Pete. "They reach for it, they pray for it, and quite often just when they need it most, they get it. It's breathed into them. That's what the word means—*spiritos*, the divine breath. Inspiration. And now it's your turn to give it back. That's how the whole thing works."

Behind the scenes, Audrey's experience in Montana, where the film was shot, mirrored her soggy moments with Fred Astaire in *Funny Face* (but without *les cygnes*). For Audrey's first scene with Dreyfuss, she had to stand on a small island of green grass with a single tree that was supposed to depict heaven on earth. It was surrounded by a forest that had burned down two years before. Down the road came Audrey's car, and almost everybody in the crew froze, because although everyone had seen Audrey Hepburn's movies, they'd never seen Audrey Hepburn in person. As Spielberg tells the story: "So you have to imagine eighty people putting on their goo-goo eyes, which immediately made Audrey very uncomfortable. After all, she wanted no special attention and I was supposed to be keeping my promise. To make matters worse, she was wearing a delicate white costume that couldn't afford even a centimeter of mud, and the only way she could make it from her car to heaven was by being carried. We all stood and watched four members of the crew hoisting her above their heads on a chair, carrying her fifty yards through the mud—like the princess she had always been in all of our dreams—right into her mark and into her key light."

BUT IT WAS NOT ENOUGH for Audrey to merely play an angel in the third and final act of her life, Audrey used her name and notoriety to help others. "Fame creates a certain curiosity," Audrey knew. "I'm using that curiosity for the children." In 1959, as Sister Luke in *The Nun's Story*, she portrayed a woman who loved God above all else. Her beautiful face glowing in the mysterious serenity of a white habit, she was dedicated to improving the lives of children in the Belgian Congo. Rob finds this movie so psychologically close to the Audrey he knew that even today he can barely watch it. The year 1989 closely mirrored her performance in *The Nun's Story*, with the real-life Audrey in blue jeans and sneakers, comforting starving children in Ethiopia.

A year before, with her sons grown, she began the job that would occupy the last five years of her life: special ambassador for the United Nations Children's Fund (UNICEF). Audrey was uniquely suited for the job, according to Wolders, since "she was a composite of reactions against bias, intolerance, and anger. Not necessarily directed toward her, but based on observation. This is perhaps why she was so even and fair with everyone. Her indignation toward intolerance grew to where there was a rage toward the injustices she observed." Audrey herself put it more simply: "I've been auditioning my whole life for this role, and I finally got it."

In her travels to Macao, Japan, Turkey, Finland, Holland, Central America, and Australia on behalf of UNICEF, Audrey's essential goodness shone through. John Isaac, an award-winning photographer who worked for more than twenty

years for the children's fund, traveled with Audrey and Rob to Ethiopia and Bangladesh. Perhaps because of the harrowing conditions they observed, often difficult for "civilians" who haven't shared their experience to imagine, John and Audrey became close friends. "Audrey was so deep and she was so sensitive. In no way would she want to offend anybody, even though there were people who were starving, and who were dying. For her, dignity was so important."

Traveling with Audrey, Isaac remembers, was memorable. Their first trip together was in 1988, to Ethiopia, when Isaac was chosen to record the event for UNICEF. "We went and we hit it off right from the beginning. She had a terrific sense of humor, so we could joke about things, and at the same time she was very sensitive." During their time together, John and Audrey discussed almost everything—John's experiences as a globetrotting photographer, poetry, and even spirituality. "We had a chat about who had the right to life. She asked me, and I said I have the right to my own life, I didn't want to be hanging on to some tube. . . . She said, 'Exactly, John, that's exactly what I think.' When she died, she wanted to die in a dignified way."

Isaac has a revealing anecdote about his friendship with Audrey—that shows, like a true aristocrat, that she never stood on ceremony but innately

followed her own vision of the "correct" thing to do. At the UN, he recalled, "a lot of the directors wanted to have lunch with her and she said no, that she wanted to have lunch with me. And if you look at it"—Isaac laughs knowingly—"I am at the lowest end of the totem pole at the UN. So the director came and said, 'You cannot accept this invitation, because all of these people will be upset because we're all having lunch at the same dining hall.' So I said, 'Look, Audrey, I will see you in the evening, when I come by for a drink.' And she said, 'Why, are you busy?' No, I said, then I explained the situation to her, and she said bullshit. You will be my escort! And we went, but that's the way Audrey was, very loyal—I was her friend, and that was it."

As her UNICEF work drew more attention, and that was, after all, part of the point, some journalists began to refer to her as "Saint Audrey." Few things annoyed Audrey, but this label truly did. Audrey was a person, after all, and calling her a saint negated her very human struggles and conceits; it overrode all her attempts at decency. "After all," she said, "I am doing only what any other human being would do." Although her actions were laudatory, Audrey was still very much one of us, as she would be the first to admit—she smoked Kents and enjoyed a glass of J&B scotch at the end of the day.

The French say that "at forty, one gets the face one deserves." In the last years of her life, now almost sixty, Audrey was most luminous when she found her final and most lasting role—that of humanitarian. Far from Givenchy's salon, the lights of Broadway, and the soundstages of Hollywood, Audrey was never more glamorous than in her later years, when she traveled simply, dressed casually, helping children few governments or people cared about. It was then, too, that she came closest to the style of an average American, but with her own distinctive twist. Her friend Eva Gabor remembers: "Nobody in the world looked better in plain white pants and a white blouse. Whatever she put on became perfectly elegant. Without a stick of jewelry, she looked like a queen."

How intriguing, how perfect, that Audrey's life came full circle: As a starving child in Holland in 1945, the United Nations gave her family much needed flour and milk. Forty-three years later she repaid in kind, traveling the world to help children who were much like herself. Fashionwise, too, she pared down the perfection of her high Hollywood glamour. Later in life, after achieving more than she might possibly have ever imagined on the stage and screen, Audrey reverted to the simple fashion of her youth, wearing cotton oxford shirts with slim pants or jeans when traveling abroad for UNICEF.

If she needed to attend an awards program (she and Gregory Peck saw each other so often at these retrospectives, they began referring to them as the "Greg and Audrey Show") or a fund-raiser for UNICEF, she generally chose between Ralph Lauren and Givenchy, instinctively returning to the classic styles she always favored. When journalists tried to invent a rivalry between the two designers, Audrey said, "It's having the best of both worlds, Hubert and Ralph. I don't want to compare them, I just want to wear them."

Although Audrey and Rob ultimately made fifty humanitarian trips in five years (never being away from La Paisible for more than two weeks at a time, since they did not like to leave the dogs any longer than that), their world was not entirely filled with UNICEF work. Holidays were sacrosanct, Christmas was always at home with Sean and Luca at La Paisible, while New Year's Eve was spent in the company of Valentino and other close friends. As Valentino recalls: "You could invite Audrey to shows, dinners, parties, she would decline most of the time. I remember when she came to the funeral of my mother, flying in just for the day. She was an angel, a very close person.

She did not need to show off her friendships—but you knew she was there."

And Audrey, it seemed, always got a kick out of the simplest situations. When she and Givenchy were both visiting Connie in Los Angeles, their favorite outing was walking to the nearby Williams-Sonoma store and buying little kitchen gadgets. Once, en route to San Francisco, Audrey had ordered a gift from Tiffany's on Rodeo Drive and stopped by to pick it up. The very young but vigilant salesperson asked, "Do you have any identification?" Audrey took off her sunglasses, smiled, and said brightly, "My face."

It was on a visit to London that Audrey and Rob's path crossed Manolo Blahnik's one rainy day on Bond Street. Blahnik recalls: "The last time I saw her, she was with that gentleman, that very beautiful gentleman, her husband, very, very elegant. And I couldn't stop staring! I was outside Sotheby's, and I was in shock, I just came out of the bookshop and I saw Audrey Hepburn waiting to get a taxi! And I was first to get one, so I just gave my taxi to her and she said, 'Oh, thank you so much, you are so kind!'" Blahnik laughs, showing that even designing stars are occasionally starstruck. "That encounter absolutely made my day!"

Like too few women of style, Audrey Hepburn, to use an old-fashioned word, persevered. Inherently shy, she remade herself at every turn in life, not to promote herself, but to fulfill her destiny. In spite of worldwide acclaim, she remained good-natured in the face of stardom and, in fact, used her celebrity to help others. She didn't fall apart or buckle under. In this respect, Audrey was like Jacqueline Kennedy Onassis, another woman of substance, who, in an odd twist of fate, fashioned her early "look" after Audrey Hepburn. And like Mrs. Onassis, Audrey reinvented herself in the third act of her life, finding love—but not marriage—with Rob Wolders.

John Loring, who befriended both women, believes that [Audrey and Jackie's] "great work of art was themselves. And the way they set an example by presenting themselves to the public, in this wonderful way that they represented what every woman should be. They were completely self-possessed, they had complete self-respect, and therefore, complete respect for other people. They never, never descended to a level that was not theirs. They were horrified by people who descended to pettiness.

"Like Mrs. Onassis, Audrey knew how to present herself as a kind of gift to the public. She did not remain Audrey Hepburn through her whole life without being very aware of what Audrey Hepburn was, and being very aware of what Audrey Hepburn had to offer the public, and that she could give the public something very remarkable to look up to and emulate, and dream about, and girls all over the world think, 'Wouldn't that be great to be like Audrey Hepburn?' Well, isn't that great? It would be a much nicer world if everyone were just like Audrey Hepburn!

"Instead of this usual modern coolness," Loring observes, "there was not coolness about these women at all. They were totally warm and feminine and open to you, and the second they started to talk to you, they were all there. This is what these women gave to people. They knew that they had a lot to give, and they were not going to hold back any of it, they were going to use it to do something for other people. Audrey and Mrs. Onassis both had a tremendous generosity of spirit, coupled with extraordinary intelligence—let's not overlook the fact that we are talking about remarkable minds, people with tremendous dimension and range too. What they were able to do—look at all that Miss Hepburn was able to do, not only as an actress, but she wrote beautifully, as a humanitarian and how she knew how to use her image for the good of people."

So we see that style is far more weighted than mere fashion. Style, in some ways, is everything. If we agree with C. Z. Guest, that style "is about surviving, about having been through a lot and making it look easy," then Audrey Hepburn's experiences contributed in no small measure to who she was, and to the woman she ultimately became. With the choices she made, artistically, personally, even fashion-wise, Audrey Hepburn transcended her early fear and loss and became part of history, joining the pantheon of style setters that women, and more than a few men, look to with admiration, possibility, and belief.

In November 1992, after returning home from a harrowing trip to Somalia for UNICEF, Audrey was exhausted and emotionally worn. Thinking she might be suffering from a virulent amoebic infection, Audrey went to Cedars-Sinai Medical Center in Los Angeles for a full checkup. It turned out, instead, to be cancer. Her condition deteriorated with shocking speed. After initial surgery to remove the cancer from her appendix and colon, it spread, just a few days later, to her stomach. Rob and her two sons were at her side; the two dogs were soon brought over from Switzerland by her vigilant housekeeper Giovanna.

Audrey decided not to undergo chemotherapy, and, remembering her conversations with John Isaac in 1988, told her family, "You can ask John, I said this way before I got sick." Rob and Sean called Isaac to confirm that this was, in fact, Audrey's wish. "Which was hard," admits Isaac today, "because I'm sure some of her family wanted her to do chemotherapy and all, but I had to say the truth, and I had to say, no, this is what she said." By the end of November, doctors determined that her condition was terminal and, short of managing the pain, nothing more could be done. After gathering her strength at Connie Wald's, Audrey had one wish: to return home and celebrate Christmas in Switzerland. Givenchy arranged for Bunny Mellon to lend them her Gulfstream jet and filled it with the flowers he knew she loved.

Before leaving, there was a final dinner at Connie's house, a place of such joy in the recent past. Audrey's closest friends, Connie, Greg and Véronique Peck, Audrey and Billy Wilder, were there. "On the face of things, we were saying good-bye because she was returning to Switzerland," remembers Peck, "but we were saying good-bye for real." Mrs. Wilder didn't think Audrey looked too bad. "She looked worn, of course, her face a little drawn, but I've seen worse . . . she was very brave. We were saying good-bye to her and we knew it was good-bye." Peck had the sense that Audrey was keeping everyone else's spirits up; "gallant" was the word he used to describe her. At one point Audrey confided to Véronique that "the pain is just awful." And she carried it off so well, she was trying to cheer everyone else up. "When I heard that in the car," confides Peck, "I practically had a lump the size of a grapefruit in my throat."

When they walked outside after dinner, there was a tabloid photographer lurking behind one of the towering palm trees on Beverly Drive, enraging Gregory Peck, who shouted at him to leave or he would call the police. "*Vulture*," spat out Audrey Wilder, wondering how the photographer could live with himself.

Hepburn's illness caught everyone off guard. No one expected this—it didn't make any sense. It was so fast. "I couldn't believe it when she got sick!" says Audrey Wilder, recalling that hard time. "What do you mean, sick? They said—*sick!* When people are younger than you and get sick, you just don't believe it! When somebody gets sick like that—it's so sudden that you don't say the last time you saw her, 'she didn't look well.' It's like—boom!—and they're dying. They're there and then they're not there."

In her final month at La Paisible, Audrey was surrounded by those she loved most, Rob and her sons. "I'm so glad I'm home," she said, "I can see my trees again." Givenchy came and spent time with her, careful not to tire her out. Doris Brynner was there every day, doing whatever she could for Audrey. "She was my heart and soul, so it was perfectly normal and goes without saying."

Audrey walked in the garden as often as she could, until stalking paparazzi took that last joy from her. As a final gift, she bought three quilted coats, one for Sean, one for Rob, and a navy blue one for Hubert. She presented his to Givenchy when he visited, touching her lips to it with a little kiss and murmuring, "Think of me when you wear it."

Rob remembers their closing days together, "That last Christmas was one of the most wonderful recollections for me. It was so important to her to have the boys and me together. We were able to sleep in the same bed until the day she died. It was just us. I remember [Audrey's] voice in the dark saying, 'This is the happiest Christmas I've ever had.'"

On January 10, Audrey took her last walk around the gardens at La Paisible, supported by Rob and Doris. She stopped at each plot and reminded Giovanni what was planted there, and the attention it would need in the spring.

"You'll be here to see it," he said to her.

She looked at him. She was as realistic about death as she was about life. Audrey did not feel dying was unjust, it was part of nature, after all. "I'll be here in other ways," she told him. At the close of her life, Audrey's thoughts were, as ever, on others. Even a few days before her death, she was trying to make Rob laugh. "She said, 'Smile for me, Robbie,'" recalls Wolders. "I tried, for her sake."

Audrey did the best she could, but finally, one day, she told Luca, "I'm sorry, but I'm ready to go." Audrey Hepburn died at home at seven P.M. on Wednesday, January 20, 1993. She was sixty-three years old. Laid to rest in a peaceful country cemetery near her home, Audrey was buried with the rings Rob and Sean gave her. "We both thought it the right thing to do," says Rob quietly. It is a testament to her grace that, in addition to the world's outpouring of grief, not only her sons, Hubert de Givenchy and Robert Wolders attended her funeral, but also both of her former husbands, Mel Ferrer and Andrea Dotti. "God has the most beautiful new angel now," Elizabeth Taylor commented memorably. And the world agreed.

HER FAMILY AND FRIENDS were devastated by Audrey's death. "She ratted on me," says Doris today, "because we had a deal that we would go together." Her leaving broke Wolders's heart. Because, of course, we think beauty and goodness—God's frailest gifts—will protect us from what fate has in store. But of course they can't, even for someone as beautiful and good as Audrey.

Robert was left, too, with the survivor's nagging question: what if? After Audrey became ill, he asked her, "Would it have been better if we had just spent the years that we had been fortunate enough to have together in Switzerland, with the dogs, with the family?" It was one of the few times Audrey became angry with Rob, because she felt this very human resquest indicated a certain selfishness on his part, and she said to him, "Think of all that we would have missed."

Still, if Wolders knew for certain that the UNICEF work might have taken away from Audrey's life, he would not have hesitated to give it all up just so she would be with them longer. Three years after her death, he accepted an award from the medical society Sigma Theta Tau on her behalf, and was characteristically eloquent and openhearted about what Audrey meant to him. "A very wise friend told me of her conviction that the time would come when the fact that Audrey lived and touched my life would be far more important than the fact that she died. That day has not quite come. The sense of loss and pain remains too intense. But there is something curious about pain. In the beginning it is an enemy, something that you don't want to deal with or face up to, but as the years go by, it becomes almost like a friend or solace. Losing someone you loved very much, the pain is unbearable, but as time goes by, you realize that it is the pain of losing them that reminds you so vividly of them. And reminds you of all that you were allowed to love.

"And what I have come to realize is that the memory of Audrey is with us today, as it will remain with us, not because she died but because she lived a life too short, that was distinguished by its humanity, long enough to leave us the message of hope, trust, with love. . . . If there is anything she would have wished for, it is that her work be continued."

Audrey lives on in the memories of those who loved her. Luca says that he thinks of her every time he passes a flower shop in Paris. "I miss the conversation," he admits. "Now if anything goes wrong, instead of getting her advice, I have to figure it out for myself." Doris Brynner confesses that she thinks of Audrey "all the time. Every day, all the time. Whatever I do I know that she would love to see it and she would be so proud of me. It's an everyday thing, and sometimes I know she's just here, so that's very good." Jeffrey Banks feels Audrey is still around, although "I still can't sit through a whole movie, I get so upset, I can't watch it." One afternoon he happened to be standing in the middle of Ralph Lauren's shop on the corner of Madison Avenue and 72nd Street, in Manhattan, of all places, when Audrey, singing "Moon River" came over the speakers. "I had to leave—I heard her voice and it was too much for me."

Although most of us are not so fortunate to have had Audrey's friend-ship, there is so much we can learn from her. In the final analysis, what Audrey Hepburn gave the world—through her grace, style, and example—was joy. As a friend put it: "One always came away from seeing Audrey Hepburn feeling happy." And as her son Sean recalls: "She believed love could heal, fix, mend, and make everything fine and good in the end."

Although she claimed not to be religious, Hepburn's outlook was inherently spiritual. She believed the purpose of life was "not to live for the day—that would be materialistic—but to treasure the day. I realized that most of us live on the surface without appreciating just how wonderful it is simply to be alive." John Isaac also reveals that Audrey "had a very philo-sophical edge to her, she read poetry, she liked Rabindranath Tagore, who was a great philosopher/poet from India who won the Nobel Prize in the 1930s." One of his lines she knew from memory was "Each child is a reminder that God has not lost hope in man."

In fact, it turns out that Audrey and John not only admired the same poet, but also shared a favorite poem. "We didn't tell each other—I told her I had a favorite poet, and she said she had a favorite too. So then we exchanged the same lines. Tagore talks about love in a way, he talks about true friendship. He says: 'May my loving you not be a burden on you, for I freely chose to love you.' And it's almost like a true love which doesn't expect anything." Given Audrey's grace and uncommon selflessness, Tagore might have been describing her own philosophy.

FROM STUDYING AUDREY'S LIFE, we see her style was exquisite because it suited her so well. She did not follow trends, but, having studied her own life and physique, chose what worked best for her. According to Wolders, "she felt strongly that elegance is in simplicity, not in opulence or sumptuousness. This conviction encouraged her contemporaries who felt that elegance was within their grasp." Like Audrey, we can develop the confidence to make the most of our assets and develop our *own* fashion instinct.

Grace. Discipline. Reserve. Simplicity. Style. What Audrey revealed on the screen or onstage is who she *was*, and in her revelations there was more grace than anything else. As Diana Vreeland so rightly noted: "Without emotion, there is no beauty." Even more than her ethereal beauty, audiences fell in love with Audrey's emotion, her modesty, her good humor and vulnerability, her strength. They could not help but admire, too, the fact that Audrey honed her gifts and garnered her talent, using them ultimately to help others. People respond to Audrey Hepburn's *goodness*, a clarity of line and thought that reflected itself as much in her choice of hairstyle as in her choice of lifestyle.

Recognizing Audrey's style, we can look for signs of it in our own lives. To create a beautiful life, as she did, is not merely to dwell on shiny surfaces, but to live authentically. At her memorial service, her son Sean remembered: "Last Christmas Eve," he said, "Mummy read a letter to us by a writer she admired. . . . 'Remember, if you ever need a helping hand, it's at the end of your arm. As you get older, you must remember that you have a second hand. The first one is to help yourself, the second one is to help others.'"

The memory of Audrey, her beauty, and all she contributed to the world—fashion perhaps being the least of it—stays with us. After her death, her son Sean said, "I still carry her every day in my heart, she is still my best friend." Givenchy, too, admitted that "in every collection a part of my heart, my pencil, my design goes to Audrey. Audrey has now departed, but I still commune with her." Knowing more about Audrey, her grace, style, altruism, and her life, we, too, can keep a small bit of her in our hearts; and impart some of her magic to our world.

Studying Audrey's life, her courage, and all she overcame can help us with choices we make in our own lives. By knowing history, we see our lives in a larger context. The courage with which Audrey faced her situations, refusing to give up, refusing to be broken by the Nazis, the disappearance of her father, or the heartbreak of her marriages, is a kind of grace. This decision to live in joy takes moral courage, and is, ultimately, one of the truest expressions of style.

shooting **a star**

"She walked in alone," remembers Steven Meisel, "wearing a blue pea coat, pants, and a pair of sunglasses. It was the most important day of my life."

Meisel was shooting Audrey at Industria Studio in Greenwich Village for the May 1991 cover of *Vanity Fair*. Meisel gathered his usual crew—Kevyn Aucoin for makeup, Garren for hair, Robert Isabell to provide the flowers—to work their magic. Audrey and Marina Shiano, the stylist, had gotten together earlier to choose the wardrobe from Ralph Lauren. It was simple. "This will work, that won't work," Audrey said, flipping through the metal racks, choosing a trim black dress, a cropped trench coat. She knew her stuff.

Meeting Audrey, the boys were as shy as prom escorts waiting for their dates. Without consulting one another, they had all dressed up in jackets and ties. Which is hilarious, in a way, if you know anything about the fashion world, because it is rare to see Kevyn Aucoin in anything but jeans and a white tank top as he rushes around backstage smudging Kate's and Naomi's eyeshadow. Even though Kevyn had told his colleagues how *wonderful* Audrey was (he had first worked with her on the Revlon shoot with Avedon), they were still nervous wrecks.

When they arrived that morning, Steven asked everybody, "Guess what Audrey wants for lunch today?"

An omelette? someone wondered. Champagne? M&M's with the red candies taken out?

"A peanut butter and jelly sandwich."

When Audrey walked in, Meisel's jaw dropped. Sixty-two years old? God, she was gorgeous! To him she seemed almost five feet ten—he had no idea she was that tall—and what a figure! "Audrey was everything I dreamed she would be," says Steven, "and then some. She was just kind and generous, and fun. A great deal of fun."

After a scurry of kisses and hellos and cappuccino orders, Kevyn got to work on Audrey's makeup while Steven took test Polaroids and discussed what he had in mind for the shoot. He wanted to give her hair a little height, but Audrey, polite as ever, refused. She had done the *Vogue* covers years ago, she reminded him, she'd done the fashion stuff, she didn't need to go back there. Meisel, who was used to remaking models into practically any image that came into his head (he had, after all, persuaded Linda Evangelista to change her hair from red to blond to brunette in practically a week), quickly agreed.

Kevyn, who also did Audrey's makeup for events like the Lincoln Center Honors, felt that "working with her was like being in the presence of someone who was not merely human. She sort of had an angelic quality about her, and a sort of ethereal, rather haunting presence. When she left, you couldn't stop thinking about her." But lest we mistake Audrey for Mother Teresa in a cashmere turtleneck: "She didn't act holier than thou, she didn't act like she was better than everyone, she just had a presence, an energy, a sort of light coming from within her that was just sort of overwhelming."

Audrey took a lipstick out of her bag, a shocking-coral color she wanted Kevyn to try. He never would have associated it with her, but in his work he doesn't tell people what they can or cannot do. So Kevyn used the coral and it looked gorgeous. One reason Kevyn loved working with Audrey was that she was *there*. Most people he dealt with were just floating through with three hundred other things on their mind. When you spoke to Audrey, you got her full attention. Kevyn was also adroit enough with the ways of celebrity to know that the public image of a famous person and his or her private image were often miles apart. When friends ask him what Audrey was like, he tells them she *was* her public image. "And that shocks them, because her public persona was so amazing that you couldn't imagine that anybody could actually be like that!"

Finally everything was ready—the lights were set, Dave Brubeck—Audrey's favorite—was cranking on the stereo, Audrey was looking *fabulous*. She stepped in front of the white paper backdrop, cradling Robert Isabell's bouquet of long-stemmed tulips in her arms, as Meisel crouched behind his camera. Everyone stood off to the side. Now it was just Audrey and Steven. He took the shot with Audrey and the flowers and, like the sight of her running down the steps of the Louvre in *Funny Face*, it was something he would never forget. "I snapped that picture and we had tears in our eyes. And it wasn't me—I just took the picture! It was totally her, it was Audrey!"

acknowledgments

THIS BOOK WOULD not have been possible without the guidance, advice, and considerable assistance of Audrey's friends, fans, and coworkers. Through them I was able to imagine her kindred spirit. Everyone spoke with me out of their continued affection for Audrey, and for their graciousness, insight, and generosity, I would like to thank: Kevyn Aucoin, Sid Avery, Ron Avery, Peter Bacanovic, Mark Badgley and James Mischka, Letitia Baldrige, Jeffrey Banks, Lina Bey, Janis Blackschleger, Manolo Blahnik, Doris Brynner, Cynthia Cathcart (Condé Nast), Rosemary Clooney, Bob Cosenza (The Kobal Collection), Stuart Crowner, Tracy Budd Day, Denise De Luca, Carrie Donovan, Caroline Dougherty, Tiffany Dubin, Katarina Feller (Christie's Paris), Mossimo Ferragamo, Pamela Fiori, Kimberly Fortier, Monroe Friedman, Hubert de Givenchy, Anne Haggerty (Condé Nast), Kym Harris (Givenchy), Campbell Lane Hart, Penelope Hobhouse, Maureen Hornung, John Isaac, Jim Katz, Wendy Keys, Michael Kors, Eleanor Lambert, Ralph Lauren, Julie Leifermann, Christopher Little, John Loring, George Malkeris, Amy Mark, Roddy McDowall, Steven Meisel, Polly Mellen, Beth Mendelson, Carol Rawlings Miller, Leigh Montville (Condé Nast), Mary Parsons, Gregory Peck, Henry B. Platt, Nancy Reagan, Christa Roth, Cynthia Rowley, Fran Silverberg (UNICEF), Liz Smith, Kate Spade, Steven Spielberg, Allen Sviridoff, Brian P. Sweeney, Faye Thompson (AMPAS Library), Christy Turlington, Connie Wald, Reid and Holly Walker, Vera Wang, Audrey Wilder, Bob Willoughby, Paul Wilmot, Robert Wolders, Henry Wolf, Stephanie Zanardi.

I would also like to recognize, and gratefully thank, all the designers who so willingly contributed their time and talent to sketch original designs for Audrey. While Audrey is a dream model, they, too, are dream designers: Mark Badgley and James Mischka, Jeffrey Banks, Manolo Blahnik, Hubert de Givenchy, Alexander McQueen, Cynthia Rowley, Kate Spade, and Vera Wang.

Audrey Hepburn's life has been well documented practically from the moment she landed on these shores to appear on Broadway in *Gigi*. I would like to express my indebtedness to the journalists, interviewers, and biogra-

phers who have preceded me: Marie Brenner, Professor Richard Brown, Nicholas Coleridge, Amy Fine Collins, Dominick Dunne, Larry King, Barry Paris, Curtis Bill Pepper, J. D. Podolsky, Stephen M. Silverman, Annette Tapert, Gore Vidal, and Barbara Walters.

I would like to especially thank maquillage master DARAC, for his inspired work within these pages, as well as Shane Powers for his evocative sketch of Audrey. I would also like to acknowledge Prescriptives for graciously providing the makeup featured in these pages.

A special thank-you to John Engstead and Steven Meisel for the stunning photographs of Audrey that grace the cover. I am in awe of their talent.

A writer without a publisher is like a farmer without a field, and I would like to thank everyone at HarperCollins for making this book possible. Deep appreciation to my editor, Joëlle Delbourgo—whose grace, insight, and ready laughter shows that Audrey is, indeed, still with us. Special thanks must also go to Roseann Glass, Joseph Montebello (who rivals Robert Wolders in the charm department), Matthew Guma, and especially Susi Oberhelman, whose talented eye for design ensured that this book suited Audrey as well as any Givenchy creation. I am also deeply appreciative of the creative vision and hard work of the marketing team led by Craig Herman, Maggie McMahon, and Kate G. Stark, who brought this book to everyone's attention. You are all a joy to work with. Perhaps it is telling that we agreed to undertake this project on May 4, Audrey's birthday (well, her *Children's Hour* costar Shirley MacLaine would think so).

I would like to particularly recognize my agent, Joanna Pulcini—whose vision, optimism, and fabulous clothes sense very much reflect Audrey Style. Linda Chester, Linda Kahn, Andrew Ayala, Gary Jaffe, Peter O'Reilly, Judith Erlich, and everyone at the Linda Chester Agency deserve a glorious Audrey bouquet for making my dreams come true. Research assistant Peter H. Saisselin was also a great help with his initiative, sense of humor, and formidable ability to speak French.

Finally, I would like to acknowledge my family, and in particular my brothers and sisters, Patricia, Peter, Terri, Deirdre, James, and Scott, whose great affection, encouragement, and laughter bring joy to my life every day. Audrey's life was full of love and because of them, mine is too. This book is for them.

photo illustration **credits**

2: The Kobal Collection

5: Original Illustration Courtesy Manolo Blahnik

6: AH wanted to eat an ice cream cone while shopping at Tiffany's, but director Blake Edwards refused. The Kobal Collection

8: Bert Stern/Courtesy *Vogue*. Copyright © 1963 (renewed 1990) by Condé Nast Publications, Inc.

11: The Kobal Collection

12: Philippe Halsman © Halsman Estate

14: Original Illustration Courtesy Cynthia Rowley

15: Original Illustration Courtesy Kate Spade

16: Original Illustration Courtesy Vera Wang

17: Original Illustrations Courtesy Badgley Mischka (left), Givenchy Couture by Alexander McQueen (right)

19: Original Illustration Courtesy Manolo Blahnik

23: AH on the set of her lone Western, *The Unforgiven*, directed by John Houston. Inge Morath/Magnum Photos

24: "The Sabrina Dress," Original Illustration Courtesy Hubert de Givenchy

27: Dennis Stock/Magnum Photos

28: The Kobal Collection

31: AH and Humphrey Bogart getting along on the set of *Sabrina*. The Kobal Collection

32: AH and Edith Head, Paramount Studios 1953. © Bob Willoughby 1999

35: *Sabrina* outfit "designed" by Edith Head. Paramount/MPTV

36: Original Illustration Courtesy Manolo Blahnik

38: Audrey with Givenchy on the set of *Funny Face*, 1956. David Seymour/Magnum Photos

41: Audrey and Givenchy walking along the Seine, 1981–1982. J. Scandeliari/Courtesy Givenchy

43: At the Glen Cove train station, Long Island, New York. *Sabrina*, 1954. Dennis Stock/Magnum Photos

47: *Young Wives Tale*, England, 1951. The Kobal Collection

48: Corbis/Bettman-UPI

51: Chorus girl, London. The Kobal Collection

52: Photograph by Cecil Beaton Courtesy of Sotheby's London

55: Audrey greeting her mother, 12/17/53, Hoboken, NJ. Corbis/Bettman-UPI

56: *Funny Face* rehearsal. David Seymour/Magnum Photos

59: *Secret People*, London, 1951. The Kobal Collection

60: AH on Wall Street during filming of *Sabrina*, 1954. Dennis Stock/Magnum Photos

63: The Kobal Collection

64: A rare Edith Head "sketch" of Princess Anne's ball gown in *Roman Holiday*. AH tested both a black and white version of the gown, but the white version "read" better on film. Courtesy of the Academy of Motion Picture Arts and Sciences

67: *Roman Holiday*, 1953. The Kobal Collection

68: AH on her first trip to Hollywood, 1953. © Bob Willoughby 1999

71: AH on the set of *Paris When It Sizzles*, Paris, 1962. © Bob Willoughby 1999

75: On her first trip to Hollywood, AH is photographed in the Paramount Portrait Gallery by Bud Fraker, 1953. © Bob Willoughby 1999

76: AH and Salvatore Ferragamo. Courtesy Ferragamo

79: AH shooting *Sabrina* on Wall Street, 1954. Dennis Stock/Magnum Photos

80: Inge Morath/Magnum Photos

83: AH posing for a fashion shoot on the set of *Paris When It Sizzles*. Director Richard Quine is behind the camera, Paris, 1962. © Bob Willoughby 1999

84: The first Hollywood photo shoot, 1953. The Kobal Collection

87: Audrey in *Ondine*. The Kobal Collection

88: Making it down the stairs without breaking her neck: AH posing for Fred Astaire in *Funny Face*, Paris, 1956. The Kobal Collection

91: AH and Famey, *Funny Face*, 1956. The Kobal Collection

92: AH posing for photographer Bud Fraker on the Paramount lot, Los Angeles, 1953. © Bob Willoughby 1999

95: © Bob Willoughby 1999

96: AH and the dreaded white socks. The Kobal Collection

99: AH and Fred Astaire on the set of *Funny Face*, Paris, 1956. The Kobal Collection

100: Paramount/MPTV

103: The Kobal Collection

104: © Bob Willoughby 1999

The most important thing is to enjoy your life—to be happy—it's all that matters.

AH

To continue Audrey's work for children,
contact your local National Committee for UNICEF.
In the United States, write the

U.S. Committee for UNICEF
333 East 38th Street
New York, NY 10016

call: 212-922-2549 or 1-800-FOR-KIDS

www.unicef.org